A Hood Tale:

BEYOND B.E.T. WITH BIG FIFTY

DELRHONDA "BIG FIFTY" HOOD

WAHIDA CLARK
P R E S E N T S
INNOVATIVE PUBLISHING

Wahida Clark Presents Publishing

1(866) 910-6920

www.wclarkpublishing.com

Library of Congress Cataloging-In-Publication Data:

A Hood Tale: Beyond B.E.T. With Big Fifty

Paperback ISBN: 978-1-957954-06-6

Ebook ISBN: 9781957954073

Library of Congress Control Number: 2022910913

Cover design and layout by: Temper Tantrum Tina & Nuance Art, LLC | Editors: Chase Bolling, Alan Nixon | Printed in United States

Foreword by Wahida Clark

As the Official Queen of Street Lit, I want to start by saying it's been my honor and pleasure to work with the legendary DelRhonda Hood, aka Big Fifty. Her story is not only inspiring but refreshingly real and unique. I don't know many that can do what she has done. Especially not with her unique style and flair! It's truly a great experience to get to highlight and celebrate a fellow queen. Like Delrhonda herself, this project was bold and ambitious. We set out in mid-May 2022 to get a book done before the Essence Festival in July 2022. It wasn't easy, but stories this good almost write themselves. With hard work and a whole lot of hustle, here we are!

My team and I are pleased to admit that we were energized by the life and adventures of Delrhonda Hood. As pioneers in literature, we had been searching for the right voice and personality to launch our newest literary endeavor, "A Hood Tale: Beyond B.E.T. with Big Fifty", the first of many exciting new projects where we infuse epic true crime stories with our signature Street Lit flava! DelRhonda is a true American Gangster whose life and testimony made her an obvious first choice. She reached a queen pin status that few -- if any -- have ever attained. That's why we had to take y'all beyond the film with the Godmother herself! -Wahida Clark

Introduction

For whatever reason you were drawn to this book, I want to say thank you for picking it up. My name is Delrhonda Hood, some people may know me as American Gangster: Big Fifty. You might have even seen the movie or the American Gangster Trap Queens special about me on BET. One of these days I'll sit down, write a memoir, and give you my real-life story. For now, I wanna take you behind the Hollywood and hood pageantry into the testimony. I've been a lot of things and wore more hats than a man covering a bald spot. I didn't have time to chase clout; I chased money and did what I had to do to make sure me and mine were straight. I did the wrong thing more times than I can count, but I'm sitting here talking to you, so I guess I did something right.

Langston Hughes once wrote "Life for me ain't been no crystal stair" in a poem called "Mother to Son". I find it powerful because in it the mother lays out how hard her journey has been while encouraging her son to continue his own with hope in his heart. It's a call to perseverance and resilience that still resonates almost a hundred years after it was written. We are a long way from the days of the Harlem Renaissance, but our communities are still rife with many of the same issues, and a few new ones besides. Now more than ever we need encouragement and reinforcement. With all this talk of microaggressions, triggering, privilege, and representation, it feels like everybody is talking about mental health, but the world gets more crazy.

When I was coming up, we didn't have safe spaces, and self-care meant washing your ass and triggered didn't have no context outside shooting people. The world is so different now, so much has changed. I can say that the pain and the anger is still the same as I'm talking to you now. My life hasn't been no crystal stair either. Shit, I don't know anyone who's had one. There was plenty of concrete, asphalt, bad tile, and maybe some broken glass though. But this isn't a sob story or pity party. Instead, this is my opportunity to speak to my fellow survivors and to those who were or are about that life. For my ex-cons, current cons, dope boys, and trap queens. If you let me, I will speak to the youth, the curious, and the old dogs still tryna learn new tricks. I want you all to feel seen and heard. I want you to know that you're not and never will be alone in what you're going through.

I bring you these words not to glamorize a lifestyle or romanticize the streets. I'm not gonna tell you to do as I say and not as I've done. It's your life, and you're going to live it as you wish. I can't promise wisdom but to share some things the movie didn't and walk you through the anatomy of the trap queen it portrayed. I can't promise I'm gonna change your life, but if I can make you think, then it was well worthwhile.

One

I COULD ALWAYS REMEMBER the old commercials that used to come on hyping up Detroit like it was the greatest place in the world. The fancy restaurants, expensive shops, ritzy attractions, and exciting skyline they portrayed looked like a dream. But even as a young child, I knew the reality. They tried to sell the dream of Detroit. Like someone handing you a shattered toy and telling you to pretend it's not broken.

My Detroit was full of broken things. Broken dreams led to broken lives and broken people. To those of us who lived in the cracks of a shattered society, it was never about that fake-ass slice of life they offered in the commercials. That's not my Detroit! In the real Detroit, it was all about survival. I should know. Detroit is my hometown. I learned how to survive, and I knew I had to get my money by any means necessary. It wasn't easy, especially for a woman. The life I lived forced me to use my gut instincts, training me to listen to that inner voice that helped keep me alive. When that failed, I resorted to violence when it was necessary. Most of all, you learned that you had to use your brain, because being smart beats being hard. Every time. I used to run these streets, at least I did in my younger days. Now rather than inspiring respect and fear in the hood, I seek to inspire the youth. I tell them my story. My name is Delrhonda Hood and in the streets, I was known as Big Fifty. I'm here to help others avoid the mistakes that I made. I'm here to save you, not just from a life of crime, but to spare you from what I went through and -- most of all -- to save you from yourselves.

I remind myself of this each time I prepare to sit down with a group of young ladies. I often see so much of myself in the faces that stare back at me: the attitude-laden scowls, masking pain, the sparkle in their eyes belying ambitious hearts, or the dullness speaking of hope lost. These young women are like a mirror. They remind me of who I am, where I've been, and where I come from. It's who I'm trying to be that gets me up and keeps me motivated to use my life story as a testimony and a lesson.

Every time I speak about my life, I'm honest about it. These girls deserve nothing less. If I don't give it to them real and in my own way, then they will never get it. It's part of my journey to help them on theirs. I've done so many things in my life. A great many had consequences I rue to this day. When I look into the eyes of the youth, I hope they know that as much as my story is meant to warn them, it's a story of redemption too. Just because you come from a broken place, doesn't mean you have to be or remain broken.

Speaking of broken, it was 1971 and my father's birthday. My mother had just taken his cake out. I can remember being ready for a piece before it was even frosted.

"It's for after dinner, Chip!" my mother had chided before asking me if I wanted to help her frost it.

It was a golden moment. One of those times you remember being special for other reason than that it preceded a storm. I could remember the bright white of the cabinets and the matching tile of my mother's immaculate kitchen. The way it seemed to make her green dress shine, and her smile was perfectly framed by the neat halo of her Afro. I sat at the kitchen table merrily frosting my daddy's cake, infected by my mother's excitement for my father's birthday.

I remember how radiant my mother seemed. She was one of those people who seemed to give off goodness like sunshine when she put her mind to it. She was fairly floating when she went back to the cabinet, and she could hear the whispering. I couldn't quite make out what was said. But I knew the bass of my daddy's voice, and my momma knew it too. Suddenly her disposition got a lot less sunny. Her face shifted from confusion to anger as she stormed from the kitchen. As my young mind pondered my mother's sudden change of mood, shuffling feet announced a half-naked woman, hair pulled back sloppily on her head, sprinting through my mother's kitchen! She looked as scared as I'd ever seen a grown-up and her distress would have been comical had I not been so confused. My father was next. Half running, half falling, he turned towards my shouting mother, torn between protecting his modesty and imploring my mama. As her purposeful steps carried her back into the kitchen with an old black pistol raised, he abandoned pleading and concentrated his efforts to escape. He scrambled for the kitchen door, mama hot on his tail.

"That's right. You better run!" she'd screamed firing at my father and the silly heifer he had brought in her house.

I flinched with every shot she took. Whether in surprise at the sound, or in fear for my daddy, I would never know. Lucky for them both my mom was a horrible shot, but it never stopped her from shooting at anyone. She returned to the kitchen, setting the empty gun on the counter with a thud nowhere near as hollow as the look in her tear-streaked eyes. She looked hurt. As the sobs wracked her frame, she seemed broken. I could remember saying to myself that I never wanted to feel like my momma looked. She sat beside me carrying the scent of gunpowder with her perfume. I sat and I hugged her as she cried, not sure of what else to do. My mama had always hugged me when I cried, and so I did the same. She couldn't see it, but I cried too, and maybe I would have cried harder if I'd have known that it would be the last we would see of my father for a while.

As hurt as my mama was, she didn't play the victim. She kept it pushing, honey, you hear me! I like to think that even if I didn't use it the same way, some of her grit rubbed off on me. Rather than mope, and throw a pity party, she packed us up, and later that day we were on my daddy's mama's porch.

"Well, I see you finally left his ass!" was my grandmama's greeting at the door.

"Mama Tilda, please!" Mama retorted.

"Well, he is my son, and he strays just like his daddy. Left me with seventeen damn kids and who knows how many mo' out there!" my mama repeated under her breath having heard it all a thousand times.

See you can love a man that ain't shit, but you don't have to take their shit. My mama wasn't keen on a lecture from a woman who had seventeen kids behind a shiftless man. Still, my grandmother took us both into her already crowded house. With so many grandkids being forced to share sucked the fun out of everything. I had loved our home and leaving like we did was less than ideal. It was in those times that I truly began to miss my daddy. Fathers are supposed to protect their families and to do that you have to be present. His failure to do so would scar me for the rest of my life.

Losing my father and my home would have been enough. Should have been enough for a young girl. I had always been such a happy child, and I tried to carry that same spirit into my grandmother's house. With my aunts and uncles and cousins, it should have been an environment filled with love. Perhaps it was, but there was darkness too. One day I found myself alone with my uncle Terry. No child should be subjected to the things he did, and the things he took from me. The vacuum created by my lost innocence, once filled with light, became a haven for anger and hostility. I was too young to understand how it changed me and how I viewed life and the world.

With my innocence gone, the desire to escape my grandmother's house grew. I imagined that if I could just go somewhere else, be somewhere else, then what was happening to me would stop. I imagined starting my life over in Hollywood. Looking back, I wanted to create a new reality for myself, and to do that I needed money.

Long before I had these big ole breasts, and I was still skinny lil Chip, I ran a lemonade stand with my bestie. Just because I wasn't Big Fifty didn't mean I didn't have big dreams and a hustle, child! Even then, I was channeling my trauma into something productive, but it didn't stop the anger. Lori was our partner, and she was supposed to be holding the money until we had hit our goal. Instead, we found out Lori had spent the money.

Hurt and angry I can remember asking her, "Why would you do this?"

Now listen here. Whenever this heifer told us that she spent our money because she wanted new clothes and tennis shoes something in me snapped. The same selfishness that had taken my innocence was manifesting itself again, this time with money. It was a violation, and child, I was tired of being violated.

Full of rage I shoved her. "You mean to tell me you're wearing our money!" I yelled.

She had the nerve to push me back, talking about some "No, I'm wearing *my* money." She pushed me back so hard I fell. Picking up a stick that seemed perfect for the job, I rose, fury in my heart as I jabbed her right in her selfish eye.

There was screaming. There was blood. There was a stick with a gooey old eyeball waving from the end like a war trophy. My mother and grandmother were shocked and mortified. First, they saw the blood, but when they saw my trusty stick, they about lost their minds. I can still hear my momma yelling, "What's wrong with you, little girl!" The look of fear and shock on her face should have hurt. Instead, it made me feel strong.

It cost my family a hundred thousand dollars for Lori's glass eye. But for me, that moment was priceless. For the first time since my uncle had taken me in the basement, I learned young that like money, violence gave me the ability to change my reality. I was too young to realize or care that it would rarely be in the ways that I would knowingly choose for myself. It would be years before people would come to know me as Big Fifty, but that day I was well on my way.

Two

I GUESS you could say that my little incident regarding the lemonade stand had my mama and them looking at me different. It felt *good* to make that selfish heifer hurt for what she had done. In those days I was asleep, dreaming that my pain had given me justification to do as I pleased. What was taken from me could never be given back. In my suffering soul there was a debt that the world had to pay. There was a song by a Detroit rock band named Power of Zeus, it was called "Couldn't Be Me", and it had a line that said, *"All I want is what's mine; I don't care who I hurt."* Y'all might be more familiar with it from the Obie Trice track *"If They Wanna Know"*. Those words resonated with me. All I wanted was what I needed and that made it mine. Whoever stood in my way had to pay the price. I couldn't have articulated any of this then. I was just angry, and I wanted change. Hence, I had to get to the money.

New age folks will tell you that money has a spirit, an energy all its own. The Bible says the love of money is the root of all evil. There's an innate truth to both. Money will become your god if you allow it. It will drive you places darker than you ever imagined where all is forgiven beneath the cold green glow of the almighty dollar.

I praise the Lord I found the truth. But at that young age, I understood that money was my ticket out of my grandmother's house. It was a promise to myself of freedom, safety, and space of my own. Money had begun to represent more than a means to pay for things. It was my means of survival, and not just materially but emotionally as well. You could say it was a fixation.

I can remember justifying maiming a young girl and pushing my family to the brink of bankruptcy with four words. *She took my money.* My family didn't understand the stakes. The malignant glittering hunger in my uncle's eyes. They seemed to shine with the promise of degradation and pain waiting for the minute I let my guard down. Before I could ever set foot on the mean streets of Detroit, I had to survive my home. A child's home should be their haven, however, instead of feeling safe, I felt hunted and betrayed. And angry, angry with my uncle, myself, and my family for not seeing what this monster in their midst was doing to me. I deserved protection, and I resolved to protect myself. Little did I know I was losing parts of the very thing I was trying to protect. My soul.

Just thinking of my grandmother's house at the time made me feel rattled and panicked. I knew I had to get out of there, every fiber of my being driving me to flee. I didn't know that the truth would have indeed set me free. Instead, I was afraid, and that fear turned into rage while hardening my heart. I fought a lot, and I always had me a hustle. That invariably led me into trouble.

After getting kicked out of so many schools, my fed-up

mother changed tack. She decided that I would enrich my morals and my faith at a good, Christian school. I also sold a *shit ton of L.S.D.* It was 1981, and I was fifteen with more money in my pocket than sense in my head. Prince was king and love was in the air. Maybe that's why *dancing ass Clarence,* with his smooth moves and even smoother tongue, had gotten all up in my head. I hadn't forgotten the example of my daddy and granddaddy, but somehow, he worked his way into my panties too.

You would have thought that my trauma and hard exterior would have kept me away from boys. Looking back at the men I chose later in life, he definitely was different than the others. But something about Clarence having goals attracted me to him. *It was sexy.* He was driven, and there's something about a man with purpose that's attractive. He wanted to graduate and dance all over Detroit. Now I know that may seem stupid now. Being a dancer doesn't seem like a viable career plan these days, but dancing in the 80s was a serious part of the culture and just three or four years later the world would get to see "Breakin'" and "Crush Groove". It required skill and dedication, and he worked so hard. He would find me when I would be out skipping class, making my rounds to dazzle me with the latest routine he cooked up. Besides, ladies, take it from one who knows, *you can't ever turn your nose up at a man that knows how to move his hips!* Gentleman, take notes as you will.

I can admit he swagger jacked on Prince kinda hard, but he was cute with it. But it was part of what made Clarence, Clarence. He wasn't afraid to emulate his idol or chase his dreams. Maybe that's why I believed him when he said he wanted to take me with him. When Clarence looked me in my eyes and said he loved me, I knew it was true. As I could understand it at the time, I loved him too. Without even knowing it, my guards came down after we exchanged those fateful three words. Before long, I ended up as so many young girls in love did, pregnant.

I can remember caressing my swelling belly while looking at my mama, and my godmother, Ms. Roberta, right in their angry faces. I was scared as hell, but I wasn't telling them that. They knew like I did that I was in no way prepared to be a mother. It didn't fit with my plans. *I wanted to make my money and party, honey. You hear me.* Having a baby wasn't no part of that.

My mama didn't like Clarence and swore I wouldn't be running behind his wannabe Prince ass. She told me I needed to focus on my baby. Just the thought filled me with terror, and with a defiant heart I told them I wasn't keeping the baby.

My godmother, my mama's resolute drinking partner, recovered from their collective moment of shock first. She pointed at me with her drink and told me that I needed to *think about this.* Like I was stupid and thinking about it wasn't all I'd done. Like it wasn't happening to *my body,* and it wasn't *my baby.* She had the most annoying habit of staying in my business. Her two cents was the last thing I wanted added to the pot. I told her as much. She thought I was being disrespectful, but to my mind, they just didn't see it. I knew in my selfishness that I wasn't capable of raising no baby. I didn't even know if I could try. My mama wasn't trying to hear that though. It was clear even then that my mother's adamance about me keeping my first child was about more than my family's Christian values. I think she saw my pregnancy as a way to save me, to curb me from my path. Something to love other than myself and my desires was just what I needed. I knew better though.

I tried to explain to my mother that I couldn't possibly keep this baby, but she shut me down. She told me flat out, I laid there and made it, and I was gonna have it!

On a certain level, I knew that nature would take its course and the baby would come whether I was ready or not. My body felt like a ticking time bomb, and I hated the way it made me feel helpless about my own fate. My mother swore to me that she would help me raise the baby, and I knew she would. As touched as I was, I knew all the help in the world wouldn't free me from the burden or the responsibility. I was trying to escape and live my life, having a baby was the exact opposite of that.

She and Miss Roberta flanked me like guardian angels. I felt their love, but it still wasn't enough to overcome my fear. I pleaded with my mother for us to find another way. Suddenly the tenderness that I'd felt radiating from my mother turned into rage.

"Damn it, Delrhonda!" my mother snapped, the end of her patience was clear on the taut lines of her face. My mother was determined that motherhood would be the lesson that finally taught me that my actions had consequences. "You're gonna have this baby, and that is that!" she roared as though she could command me into labor with the power of her words alone. I knew I was gonna have to have my baby anyway. I was too far along.

After Rodney was born, my mother held true to her promise. She worked and took care of my baby like it was her own. Maybe I struggled with postpartum depression, or maybe I just truly wasn't ready. Whatever the reason was, I had a difficult time connecting with my firstborn child leaving my mother to do most of the work. She was exhausted and fed up. It seemed like her plan for motherhood to make a responsible woman out of me had backfired. In my selfishness, I never realized then, that I was repeating a cycle with my mother. Unwittingly I had let my feet follow the same footsteps of my father, leaving her once again for all intents and purposes a single mother. By the time I managed to bond with my son, my mother was too emotionally exhausted to care, and I was too caught up in my own shit to notice.

Clarence ghosted us after Rodney was born. That made it especially hard to navigate since I was having trouble navigating being a teenager and a mom. Motherhood is trying even with a loving partner and support, and I'm not ashamed to admit I struggled. Being a mom is as much about mindset as it is biology. It requires a discipline and a patience that I had yet to grow into. The same survival instincts that I had honed to survive my childhood proved to be an obstacle to me as I attempted to be a mother for the first time.

I knew that I might not be able to be the kind of mother that my own mama expected me to be, or maybe even the mother that Rodney deserved, but I knew I would provide. Hustling came naturally where motherhood didn't, and I knew that I would do what it took to give my son the things my mother couldn't afford to give me. With that revelation, the streets called me louder than ever before. Rather than focus on what I had at home, my mind shifted to my first love. *Money.* The only difference was now I had a new justification for my grind. *I had a mouth to feed.*

Motivated and hungry, I enlisted my homegirls. Melanie had mastered the world's oldest profession. My mama called her White Girl, simply because it got under her skin. Then there was Monica, who folk called Terrible Tee in the streets. She'd always been my camera in the streets, keeping me apprised of what's going on like my own hood CNN. Not only did they rip and run the streets with me, but we kicked it when it was time to lay low too. Now that I think about it, they probably spent just as much time in my room at my mama's house as I did.

Together we would ride the highs and lows of the street life. I wonder with the blessings of wisdom and hindsight if my home girls would do it all again. Your guess is as good as mine, because sometimes I think we just had too much fun. We lived life to the max, each and every day.

If we could have done it productively, applying our God given gifts in more meaningful directions, the sky would have been the limit. At many points, we face crossroads. Nexus points that allow us to take our lives forward, to the side, or even backwards. Knowing which way to go might never be easy, *and you shouldn't expect it to be if you have a lick of sense.* But the one thing you must never lose sight of is the fact that as long as you're willing to do the work, there's always options.

As for me, while I have regrets, I don't think I'd change a thing. When I hit this particular turning point in my life, I made the choices I made -- for better or for worse.

Three

SO MANY TIMES, I look back at my life, the choices I made, and the people I hurt. Justification is a funny thing. It's easy to be like, y'all know who the fuck I am and how I get down, so why cross the grain? It's cause and effect. Most people who don't fuck around, never have to find out. It was so simple. So, when I was running the streets, it was easy to write off the things I had done.

Now let me be clear. I'm far from the one to tell you that there ain't a chain of fools out here that need their ass whooped. That would be crap. I think that just as it says in the Bible, there's a time and a place for everything. Even violence. That doesn't mean that I condone the bullying, senseless killing, or any of the bullshit. I just think that some-times a foot in the ass is what the doctor ordered sometimes. I took my foot to a lot of asses over the years. Some things I might have me a good chuckle about, but other times my heart fills with regret.

I've accumulated the wisdom to know that conflict is a part of life. But it's what you do in moments of conflict, how you handle it, that defines who you are in this world. There's plenty of occasions where all I could do is play the hand I was dealt. Everybody gotta do what they gotta do to survive. I will never apologize for defending me and mine, but I recognize when I crossed the line. At the end of the day, it's about control.

If you know you know. There's nothing in the world like whooping somebody's ass to make you feel like you're in control. The only thing better may be getting the drop on somebody with a gun. I mean, who doesn't like to be a winner? The moment itself could be better than sex. Your adrenaline is going, and you watch your enemy's eyes fade from fight to fear. You have the power. Look at you, you are the captain now. You're in control? But who is controlling you?

That's a question I never asked myself when I was letting the complex web of emotions make my decisions for me. Anger can be a useful emotion, a tool just like anything else. It's when you become a tool for your anger that you have a problem. The hard part about it is, that it's difficult to stop. Anger and bitterness are like parasites on the soul, eating away at our lives and sanity. I can say that now, but I'll be damned if I could see it then. My perspective only let me see what I saw at the time.

Like I said before, if you don't dig too deep it's simple cause and effect. Cause, somebody did some clown shit to set me off, and effect. I would effectively correct their ass with whatever I could get my hands on. Slapping the shit outta people was cool, but pistol whipping was better Fucking up my hands and nails was not the wave. To put the icing on the cake, I was good at it. That didn't change the fact that there were plenty of times when exerting my control over a perceived enemy, that I really lost control over myself. In the streets, those are the types of moments where names are made and legends are born.

As far as legends go, trust me, I was well on my way. Walking home with an eyeball on a stick for a trophy was a hell of a statement. Could you imagine a better way for me to announce to the streets who I was? Anybody who knew something about it would tell you Lori played with my money and then had the audacity to jump bad with me. You could say that event was the seed of who I would become, and maybe that's why that story fascinates people to this day. I can say after that I got more than my fair share of fearful looks around the neighborhood and even from my family. I don't even think I minded. Something about instilling terror in other people made me feel big where my uncle's abuse had made me feel small. Wrapped up in it as I was, I couldn't see the secret hand of my unhealed trauma guiding my strings like a puppeteer.

I wish I could say that taking Lori's eye wasn't the only time I scarred someone for life before I turned eighteen. Shit, the way I saw it if somebody out here whooping ass and taking out eyes, I'd stay out their way. I mean you would think that after turning ole girl into a cyclops people would have fell the fuck back and left me alone. But they didn't. Some people are just plain ignorant, crazy, or too hard-headed to care. After a while it got exhausting, but back in those days, I just wished somebody would try me. It didn't matter where we were, or who was watching, I was setting it off. In my mind at the time, there was no other option. That was the best way to handle it.

Those that know, in the streets, violence -- or the threat of violence -- is like a credit score. The higher it is, the easier it is to get what you want. When it's low...well we know how that goes.

Violence and poverty are family. Together they create a vicious cycle born from broken lives and broken homes with broken dreams fed by living in a broken system. The only human reaction to that is sadness, frustration, and anger. Some people find ways to channel it. That's why sports and music are such common dreams. Others are forced to choose a punching bag, yourself, or the world around them. I chose the world. I'm not quite sure when I made that decision, but I've been blessed to live long enough to gain the insight to know one thing. I'm not the only one that paid for it.

Even when I wasn't looking for trouble it seemed to find me. After the incident with Lori, I had to switch schools. The problem was this was Detroit. In the Motor City, different neighborhoods came with different gangs, and where you lived mattered. Unfortunately for me, my new school landed me in the middle of some neighborhood beef.

Barbara Jordan, where I attended school was the domain of the Sista K's. Normally, I didn't have time for it, but they wanted all the smoke and, as one of their compatriots would learn, I had it for 'em. Every group has its resident shit starters. Now folk with sense avoid people like that, but sometimes you can't, and that's when shit gets real.

After all the trouble behind Lori and her eye, I had done my best to keep my cool. Ignoring set trippin' is rough, especially when raggedy heifers is talking down on you, your hood, and your mama. I was always the type to trade blows over insults, and ignoring people only gets you so far. A Sista K named Lorenda Lashay had decided that she would be all about giving me shit. I guess she figured living next door to my grandmama gave her easy access. She would learn that there wasn't a damn thing easy about me, the hard way.

One day after school I was at my grandmother's house, minding my business. It was beautiful outside, and nobody seemed to want to be indoors. Funny how those days and trouble always seem to go together. Perhaps if I took my ass in the house things would be different. If Lorenda would have kept her mouth shut, things would have worked out just fine. Instead, she had to start with her bullshit.

The exact contents of her tirade are lost to me now; all I can remember is that they were horrible, and they had hurt. That hurt became shame and then anger. Especially with my grandmama looking on. Not only were Lorenda's words cruel to me but towards my grandmother as well. I saw this odd look on my grandmama's face as Lorenda escalated from verbal abuse to outright threats. A deep fury rose up and washed away in my sense in a flood of rage.

What happened next, I can never forget. Lorenda charged my grandmother's porch like a mad bull, nothing but pure murder in her eyes. I was more than ready for her ass. With one look at the high railing that sat astride my grandmother's porch identical to all the other neighborhoods, I leaped it. Lorenda and I met as soon as her feet hit my grandmother's property line, fists flying. Now let me say this, Lorenda might have run her mouth, but she had the heart to back it up. I respected her for running up, but it wouldn't save her. We traded blows toe to toe, but what Lorenda would realize is that I was built for this shit. With a couple of well-placed punches and some shoves, we ended up on the ground. We scrapped furiously amongst the broken masonry that always seemed to mark the property lines.

I didn't know what I had ever done to Lorenda to justify her fury. All I knew at that moment was that she had crossed the line. First with talking shit, then again with running up on me. The brick appeared in my hand as if it by magic. It fit like it belonged there like I had always been meant to hold it, and it was left there just for me. There was no magic in what came next, just fury. I took that brick and I smashed Lorenda upside her head with it. I felt the shock of the impact travel up my young arm. It felt good, it felt wrong, but it felt *right* too. I saw her rage turn to shock, pain, and, eventually, fear. Then I hit her again.

Lorenda's mother had been coming up the street. I don't know if she heard the argument or saw the *whole* fight. I do know she saw me descend like the hand of God with that brick on her daughter.

"Oh my God, my baby, my baby!" Lorenda's mother screamed as she came tearing up the street. "Stop her; she's killing my baby!" she wailed, hysterical and desperate for the fight to end.

By that point, I had stopped, but it was too late. Lorenda was a mess. I knew she was alive because her breath came in weak, wet gasps that rattled through the blood and snot on her face. She wasn't moving though.

"You done killed my baby!" Lorenda's mother screamed as she arrived on the scene.

My grandmother and them were already trying to get me in the house. I remember letting the brick, now sticky with blood and maybe a little hair drop. I felt tired and drained; the adrenaline faded -- fear and elation mixed with morbid fascination as I looked down on my victim. Just moments ago, she had been vibrant and talking shit.

Seeing Lorenda stretched out was like seeing a candle

snuffed from a bright flame to an ember on a wick. I'd like to say something in me changed after seeing her like that, but that would be a lie. Instead, I maybe felt a little numbness tinged with a grim satisfaction that them little bitches at school would think twice before running their mouths to me again. They rushed Lorenda away in an ambulance; her mother was beside herself with grief. She knew then what I wouldn't find out till later. Lorenda would never be the same again.

My family was frantic, insisting that we would have to move because of what I had done. It didn't register how serious it all was when I'd first watched the ambulance rush her away. It still didn't fully click after Lorenda returned from the hospital after what seemed like a long time. I can admit, she looked crazy with her head bandaged up like an accident victim from the cartoons. In my mind, it had been a fight, and I had come out on top with the help of a handily placed brick.

It was almost a year later when the true cost of that fight hit me. I was pregnant with my first, Rodney, and I was out at a party. This chick rolls up *talking shit.*

"Oh, you don't remember me? Look at you, pregnant, what are you like fifteen? I guess your mama and them ain't got no control over you."

Now I may have been on the fence about motherhood, but I knew my pregnant ass didn't have no business fighting. I'm glad I listened rather than throwing hands. This girl turned out to be Classy, and Lorenda was her sister.

" Do you know my sister walks up and down the road *talking to herself?* She ain't been right since you hit her!"

I could tell the girl was mad and if I wasn't pregnant, she

would have fought me. Her disgust stung, as did knowing that a simple neighborhood beef had ruined this girl's life.

I couldn't help but think of the life I had growing inside me. I remembered the horror of Lorenda's mother the day of the fight. Even to this day, it's things like this that trouble my spirit. All the apologies in the world won't bring back Lorenda's mind. A five-second act of violence had destroyed a lifetime of potential. If I could go back and do it again, I would have still fought her. She ran up on me, and I don't think I had a choice, but I probably wouldn't have picked up that brick. *I for damn sure know I wouldn't have hit her so hard.*

That wouldn't be the last time I would be confronted by my victims or their family. Years later my heart would break again. It turns out that Lori lost way more than an eye. Her people had gone to my grandmother's house looking for me. Rather than revenge, they wanted answers. They wanted to know *why.* As I said before, on the surface it all seems so simple. But is a few dollars of lemonade stand money worth an *eye?* I could say it wasn't about the money; it was the fact that she violated our trust and friendship and then attacked me when I confronted her. Depending on your personal level of petty, you could call it karma., but I know now that the Jesus in me is bigger than that.

Lori losing her eye set her on a spiral of depression and self-loathing. Her appearance was important to her and when she lost an eye, she lost the part of herself that believed she was beautiful. Her spiral ended in addiction. Losing an eye was something she never got over. Her inability to recover from what I took from her was her destruction. No, I didn't destroy her mental capacity like I did Lorenda, but I did ruin her capacity to love herself. None of us sitting here can determine the true human cost to either woman. With a heart full of contrition, I have to live with that.

Looking back, I was still reacting to the trauma of what my uncle had put me through. I couldn't punish him but, I could punish anyone else who crossed me. It's the trickle-down economics of trauma. That pain bred rage that I still struggle with to this day. Abuse is cyclical. When we allow our unhealed pain to become rage, if we aren't careful, we become abusers. Some turn it inwards and struggle with addiction or cutting, others victimize their own relatives like my uncle did to me. Then there are those of us who vent that poison on the world. You can excuse any act when you hate yourself because it allows you to hate the world by extension.

It's easy to say shitty things were done to me, and that absolves my shitty behavior. But in order for anybody's pain to matter, in order to heal, you have to rise above that. Otherwise, life becomes a game of kick the can, each of us trapped in an echo chamber of our own pain until we all drown in an ocean of interconnected trauma. If I could say anything to my younger self, it wouldn't be make better choices. *No,* I would tell little Chip as I was known then to make her own choices rather than letting my trauma make them for me.

Four

YOU EVER WONDER why it seems like every time, you get yourself in a groove, the wheels fall off? Like seriously. That's that bullshit. Just because I had given up on being the traditional mother of the year to Rodney, didn't stop me from doing my thing to become hustla of the year. Unfortunately for me, moving and shaking in these streets was a nighttime gig. That's exactly what got me fucked up.

My momma and I had developed this routine. She would wake me up in the morning fussing and complaining. I would push the covers back, sit up, and pretend like I was up and alert. I'd do that just long enough for her to leave. Before my mama's back tires hit the bottom of the driveway, my ass went back to sleep. Now my baby, Rodney, he wasn't nothing like me. He was diligent, he worked hard, and hated being late. A few minutes after my mama, he would come pitter-pattering in the room. His hair and teeth would be brushed, and he'd be fully dressed. Ready for school in a way I couldn't even understand.

"If you don't wake up mama, I'm gonna be late. " he'd say.

Now, the first time I blew him off, to catch a few more minutes of sleep; oversleeping had been an accident. I woke up in a panic to an empty house. Took me a full two hours to realize the car was gone too. So, by the time my mama and the school found out, Rodney had been driving himself for weeks. Go ahead and laugh. It's funny, even though it's not really funny. Still never did find another child that would rather risk a whooping than be late for school. Just saying.

As chuckle worthy as it was, my mama wasn't laughing. I was used to her being angry, but this was something entirely different. I'd screwed up and messed around and my mama's bark had always been worse than her bite. But the fact that I had knowingly endangered her grandbaby, so I could sleep. Shit, just thinking about the look on her face makes me want to slap the taste out of my own mouth, even after all these years.

It's messed up how you can love somebody and not see the wrong you do. If I would have had my priorities in their proper order, I would have known better. The bottom line is, Rodney's little ass might have been a better driver than I was, but as his mother, my first instinct should have been to protect him. He had a mother that loves him; he shouldn't have had to drive himself to school. Caught up in my perspective as I was, I didn't see any of that. Rather than apologize, I accused my mother of overreacting.

I think that was the breaking point. The vein, you know the one all angry mothers have, well it throbbed, swelling with enough force that I thought her head might explode.

"I cook, I clean, I wash, I mother your child." my mama raged, with enough force I had to avert my eyes.

Each word felt like a slap. I had been chilling, smoking and drinking with my friends, and only half-listening. If I had been just a tad bit more self-aware, I would have seen how fed up my mother truly was. She really didn't ask me for much. I couldn't see how ungrateful I must have seemed when I failed to do the simple things she asked me to do. A lesser woman would have written me off a long time ago. I think all my mother would have needed to see was just a little bit of contrition and things might have turned out differently.

When you're young, you never recognize the moments where you push your life in the wrong direction. There's a reason people lucky enough get to an age where they say the youth is wasted on young people. It sounds right, but I don't think it's true. I think maybe circumspection is wasted on the old. I couldn't see past the walls I was forced to build, and my mama didn't know what I had been through. Miscommunication often leads to tragedy, and it did.

A life of being mad for my own reasons made it all too easy to react with my typical attitude. What I was really thinking and feeling at the time, any apology that might have formed was lost in a deluge of hurt, as lost as poppin' off at the mouth. The thunder in my mama's face let me know I had stepped in it. I could feel it squish by the way she told me to *"Get my shit and get out!"* My mama gave me till the count of ten without a single trace of love or empathy. It was the same look she had in her eye when she chased my father out. My ass got to packing my things, and I put my friends to work knowing my mama was stomp a mudhole in anybody's ass serious. I'm not even joking when I say that I think I set a record for world's fastest move-out. Shit, I had them bitches stuffing bags like we was working in the dope spot. The entire time, I was sweating trying to figure out where me and Rodney would go. Everything was packed and I was just about to call for Rodney when my mother came sauntering in my room with Rodney and my godmother in tow. From the hard set of her shoulders and the dangerous glint in her eye, my alarm bells started ringing.

"Aren't you gonna say goodbye to your son?" she asked belligerently.

I couldn't believe the words that were coming out of her mouth. "It's you that needs to say goodbye; Rodney is coming with me!" I shouted back. I hadn't for one second considered that I would be leaving without my son. My mother's cold glare was brooking no arguments, but I wasn't going out without a fight.

"*You done lost your ever loving mind,*" my mother retorted sadly.

I told her he was my son, but it sounded weak, even to my ears. I clutched at Rodney's shoulder's, holding him close as though it would stop the inevitability of her next words.

"He's staying here!" my mother stated with a finality I couldn't touch.

"You can't take her son!" Melanie shouted, jumping bad with my mama, trying to defend me. It would have been heartwarming, if I didn't see her life flashing before my eyes. My mother turned her anger on her. Daring her to say another word and punctuating her challenge with *White Girl*. Melanie couldn't help herself, immediately defending her Blackness and all but guaranteeing my mama would get her gun.

At that point it was time to go. My mama wasn't afraid to let it wave and squeeze the trigger. I knew I was more likely to wind up dead than walking out with my son. I loved my mama, and she loved me. That didn't change the fact that she couldn't shoot worth a damn, and if she started firing in that room, she was just as likely to hit me as Melanie. I was too young and fine to die in the process of my mama trying to do for her hated White Girl. I might have been a little crazy, but I wasn't stupid -- neither was Melanie. When mama chuckled and told Melanie to stay right there, we knew it was time to go.

Life is gonna get crazy. It's going to throw things at you. That's where you decide who you are and make your choice. Either you roll with the punches and boss up, or life will beat you down. We can't control what comes our way; we can only plan and make our choices. The one thing in this life you have absolute control over is your attitude, and that's what separates the real winners from the losers in this life. Yes, my mama had thrown me out, and I didn't have a real place to live. After what I had already been through, I had every excuse to run to drugs or bury myself in a bottle. Instead, I chose a different path.

In retrospect, I had finally gotten what I always wanted, freedom. Without a real plan or a place to go, I ran to the streets like Moana ran to the water -- except I didn't dance on the shallows or skim the surface in a cute little boat. No, I dove in with both feet. The streets rolled out a concrete carpet and I let it take me straight to the fast life.

In case you haven't worked it out by now, I'm radically honest. So, I'm going on to tell you straight. Yeah, some bands made me dance and do a little more besides. Now it may not be for everybody, but sex work, *is work. Being technical about it, stripping is a lot more effort than busting it open.* I will tell anyone in the industry that as long as you respect and protect yourself, there is no reason to be ashamed of it. You're a service provider, just like Netflix, or T-Mobile. Keeping things on hundred, prostitution is a lot more honest than most folks' jobs. I mean you might fuck a prostitute, but you ever hear people out here saying, "Fuck prostitutes!" like they say "fuck the police"? People think it's all about shaking ass, being cute, and having sex. It's not all orgasms and lube, though. The truth is, when you become a sex worker, you're a therapist, cheerleader, sex object, and a diary. For some, you might even be a lifeline to human contact. People will tell you about themselves, their lives, or just their day, and you might be the only person in the world that at least pretends to care. If you're in the business and you're paying attention, you realize you're not really selling sex, you're selling a temporary cure to loneliness. I like to think that although people look down on it, sex work properly executed brings -- if not happiness -- then fulfillment and relief. The exploitation is a mutual thing, and not many people can say that about the work they do.

I'm not saying it was always fun. I'm not gonna lie to you and say that it was easy. Anything that brings you into contact with people can be draining both on body and spirit. I'm not saying it was my best choice, but sometimes the only choice you have is the best choice you're gonna get. For a lot of women, sex work would have been rock bottom. As far as things go, I can think of worse gigs to get a woman on her feet. Sell a man drugs, he might overdose. Sell a man some liquor, he might get drunk and kill somebody. *Sell a man some ass though*...what's the side effect other than sleep and lighter pockets.

With my aunt showing me the game and keeping me safe, I was able to use a fine set of headlights and my sparkling personality to maximum effect. Soon popular with customers, and even some of the other girls, I put my hustla's spirit to work, and soon I was running a brothel of my own. As the boss, *customer service* wasn't something I had to do *unless that bread was right!* My ladies were beautiful, my in-call spot was comfortable, and the money came rolling in. I *never* let our patrons get out of line, and I made it a point to protect the women around me like a lioness. I had leveled up from that high school girl slanging LSD. For the first time ever, I became a boss in the world of the streets. My time running my brothel taught me valuable lessons that would serve me well later as I rose to power in the street.

Five

⟋⟍

OFTEN TIMES we look at the people who ground us as restraints, when really, they are anchors that keep us from a fate like Icarus. Out of my mama's house and on my own, I started really rocking. With my brothel operation earnings, I spread my wings and the streets truly began to learn that I was nothing to fuck with.

The reasons were simple. I didn't let nobody play with me and mine. I don't think it really sank in until the night Small Time pissed me off. Now things had been cool; he was my people because If we needed something done in the streets, he would do it for free. His thing for Melanie made him loyal and reliable. One mistake was all it took.

We were chilling burning L's sipping a bottle in my black Infiniti. Mel was in the back seat with Small Time. He must have been feeling himself in his plush little fur and Coogi sweater, chains glinting on his neck. When he got slick with Mel, she got slick right back, and then he did some clown shit and hit her. All the little work he put in for me flew out the window with the blunt smoke as we all started going off at the same time.

Monica and Mel jumped out. "Get your punk ass outta the car!" Mel roared, reminding us of why they called her Terrible Tee as she hauled open the door and dragged Small Time out the car like he was a bag of groceries. Small Time tried to pretend like he didn't know he had fucked up. Maybe the fool was too drunk and high, or maybe he thought that it was fine for a man to put his hands on a woman. I don't care if you're drinking moonshine and high off Molly, as a man there's no excuse to put your hands on a woman. Any man that does it makes himself less and all other men less in the process. I *knew* he was faded, but the very idea that Small Time had just hit Mel, and the fact that he did it so casually and subconsciously, left me enraged. You wouldn't have known it though by how I rose up out of my car. On the surface, I was calm and collected. Inside, though, it was like a cold fire had taken residence in my heart and burned through every limb. I let my homegirls do all the screaming. You see, Small Time might have hit Mel, but he had struck a nerve with me, and his ass was gonna pay.

By the time I got out the car, Monica and Mel were already running his pockets. I sauntered over. Small Time was rocking shades, but they could hide the terror I saw on that man's face. The confusion had turned to anger, but I watched it melt away. A Detroit gangster was reduced to a sniveling little punk before I even raised my gun. *You could've built a bridge across the lake with the bricks that nigga shit.* It was almost like I could taste his fear, and it fed a darkness that compelled me to make this fool pay.

Monica looked at me. "Whatcha wanna do, Chip?"

She didn't need me to tell her shit; she'd been handling it just fine.

I kept him pinned under the malicious eye of my gun while Mel had gotten his jewelry and Monica had gotten his cash. Her question wasn't for instructions, Monica knew me, knew how I got down. This was an invitation, and I took it. "I say we kill 'em." Small Time didn't do himself any favors.

"Yall just gonna rob me and leave me! Y'all some dirty bitches!" he cried on the verge of tears. That was it.

Something in me snapped. *"Dirty bitches!"* I screamed indignantly as Small Time cowered before me. My gun was already moving, colliding with his shiny head with a meaty this. [???] *I pistol whipped the shit outta that clown.* When he fell to the side, I stood over him screaming, "Who's the bitch now?" Mel and Monica looked on smiling in approval at how I handled his coward ass.

"Please don't kill me! Please don't kill me!"

I looked down on the sniveling wretch and asked him, "Who's the bitch now?" I spat as my finger inched toward the trigger, itching to squeeze. Part of me was itching to end him. I could almost feel the weight of the trigger as it pulled. I imagined the acrid taste of the gunpowder in the air and the way the gun would buck in my hand. I could see the look of shock forever left frozen on his face before my round tore it away.

To this day I don't know why I let him live. Maybe an angel whispered his name in God's ear, because on a whim I stayed my hand. We left Small Time's soft ass bleeding in the parking lot. Detroit would soon learn a queen had arrived.

My next flex was busting checks. It required a little organization and a head for numbers, but my time in the brothel had sharpened my business senses. Back before computers, Excel, and the internet, we had to keep a *paper* ledger with names, addresses and phone numbers just to keep track. Being organized helped us avoid mistakes that would get us caught up. Defrauding the government ain't no joke. *Uncle Sam is gang-gang about his money!* Still, it's not surprising that check fraud is one of the most common types of bank fraud. You see *now* debit cards are the thing, but *back in the day!* Checks were a literal gold mine.

There were a bunch of ways to bust a check back then. Paperhanging was simply opening an account just to be able to write bad checks. *That was basic.* Check floating, where you buy a little time, usually a few days on a bad check. Check kiting where you send money to and from accounts via check withdrawing the available funds before the bank can catch on. A check mule would accept a phony check and cash or deposit it, then wire the money for a cut. *Sometimes* folk are just old and they die but nobody says nothing and their checks just kept coming in the mail. If somebody happened to collect and cash those checks...*oops*.

We were clearing thousands a day. Maybe one of these days I might tell y'all exactly how I did it. Safe to say that some of the tax returns we were submitting to the government weren't precisely, technically, real. But fuck the government and fuck the Federal Reserve and fuck the Internal Revenue Service too. If you're stealing from thieves, is it really theft or just reallocation? Look up fractional reserve banking, and you will see what I mean.

. . .

Anyway, not only was it lucrative, it was easy, too. A white-collar gig could fly below the radar if you did it right. It beat freezing my ass off on a corner in the winter and sweating it off in the summer. It also came with a lot less drama. A victimless crime, unless you count the government, and Uncle Sam ain't no stranger to crime. As low key as it was, the check game didn't mean I still wouldn't have to get my hands dirty. After all, you can always expect people to do the human thing.

One day I'm going over the books with Melanie, and the count was off. Our system was simple but effective. I would read off a name, and Melanie would cross-reference it with a check and a wad of cash. When I called the name Dawn Miller and Mel didn't have a check, we had a problem.

Hopping in the car, Mel and I sped to the address from the paperwork. When we pulled up there was a skinny Black chick outside raking leaves like she didn't have a care in the world. I guess she didn't know that playing with my money also meant she was playing with her life. *We pulled up on her ass like the jump-out boys!* When I jumped out the car, gun low in my hand, she froze with eyes as wide as plates in her shocked face. I don't know what she thought was gonna happen, but her whole face said *she knew she fucked up.* Everyone who has ever caught anyone doing something shady knows the look. *One part guilt, three parts oh shit.* She choked up on the rake, clutching it tight like it was gonna fly her to safety.

. . .

I came around the car talking to her like I was her mama. "Dawn Miller! You know you know better!" I snapped. Dawn raised a hand, her entire body shaking like a leaf. Her lips moved but, whatever she was gonna say, was lost as I uppercut her ass with my gun. She had the nerve to spin like a whole ragdoll and she hit the ground. From the pain in my fingers radiating from my broken nail told me immediately it has been a solid shot. My skill in pistol-whipping was a double-edged sword. I saved money on bullets just to spend it in the nail salon.

After that, she was done playing stupid. I sent her in the house to get my money; I sent Mel with her to make sure Dawn kept any further stupid impulses in check. I waited outside lamenting my next trip to the nail salon and the side-eye that I would get from the nail techs. I can admit, it was risky running down on Dawn Miller. Anything could have happened, but I didn't see it like that. Far better to lose her revenue than to create an enemy who would snitch or send some people looking for me. You never know who's watching or who somebody knows. You never know which reaction is gonna get you caught up. But I wasn't thinking about any of that. I was more worried about the thirty to forty checks we cleared a day.

With the money I had coming in, shopping became my therapy. Now I couldn't be walking around in no basic shit from Macy's, so I played the boutiques hard. Something about being in those fancy stores made me feel closer to the dream of the ritzy Detroit the tourism video showed. Fashion became a way I could express myself. Some women wrote poetry, others may draw or paint. I know more than a few ladies that can sing the rafters off of any building they set foot in. *For me,* I had my body as a canvas and Chanel and Luis Vuitton as my paint. There's something about looking good that makes you feel good. No matter what's going on with you on the inside, you can always make sure the outside is top-notch. It's a sense of control, a way of bringing order from chaos, and that was a vibe for me. While maybe not as effective as going to a real therapist, the retail therapy always made me feel better. My mother and grandmother might not have been able to afford to shop in places like Hudson's, so *I would shop at Saks to flex for them!*

One day out shopping with Melanie and Monica. I could feel the money burning a hole in my pocket, and shopping with my girls was a perfect way to blow off steam. *Lord knows how much trouble the store kept me out of.* The racks were packed with brands my ratchet-ass friends weren't used to at the time. Yves St. Lauren and Christian LaCroix didn't precisely roll off their tongues. It used to work my nerves to be out there tryna ball with some class and their asses couldn't pronounce nothing.

By the time Monica and Mel had annoyed me, I realized that we hadn't been served. *Like at all.* The little clerk didn't even come around with the little *"Can I help you..."* that translates as *"What the hell are you coons trying to steal?"* With the way they ignored us we could have boosted that bitch blind and been gone, *had I have been of a mind.* Instead, my mind was on a couple cute things I had found. I had me a little outfit in mind and money to burn and I was not to be denied.

. . .

Luckily for me and maybe unfortunately for the little clerk, Monica and Melanie was with the shits. I heard Mel clear her throat and in her best impersonation of what we all know as a *Karen* today she said, "Umm excuse me!" She was joined by Monica bellowing a loud ass "Hello!!!" I started to laugh. I looked at Mel and Monica. *"Y'all know that heifer hear you!"* I told them. Now, I could have told them to pipe down, but they wanted to treat us like we was ghetto trashy, so why not act up a little?

I looked around until I saw the clerk. "Yoo-hoo, can we get some service over here?!" in my own best Karen voice. The clerk's face started to flush as other customers started to leave. Her hands seemed to twitch a little as fighting to smooth the sharp little crimson dress she wore. I almost felt bad until she had the nerve to put her fingers to her lips and shhh me. Now I could have slapped the color off her dress, but I was tryna be cool. *That didn't change the fact that I had a point to prove.*

After condescending to acknowledge our presence by shhhhing three grown women, she added insult to injury with shitty customer service. "Could you guys turn the volume down?" she gasped dramatically. "You're making the other customers a little uncomfortable." she snapped at us. Mel and Monica were still sputtering about being shushed.

The rudeness was astounding. Now, ain't a living soul ever found me to be nondescript. *She had to know we were there.* Being ignored had made me uncomfortable. After all, here I was, a brown woman trying to spend some green-ass money. Fact of the matter is, the dollar is only almighty when people think you have it. Rather than freak out on her ass, I smiled.

I wish you could have seen the way her face paled. That clerk could probably see it in my eyes that I was ready to whoop her ass from one end of the store to another. But this was society, not the street. Instead, I summoned a voice dripping with false sweetness and faker than I ever used with any John and said, "I don't care about any of that." *Just to match her energy.* Then I had to turn up on her, "AND WE'VE BEEN IN HERE LONGER THAN ANY BITCH IN HERE!" I shouted, letting a little of the hood creep into society. "We've been here longer than that ho, over there!" I continued pointing at a woman I had seen the clerk serve. "And I for damn sure know I been here longer than that trick over there! I said pointing to a woman with an entourage. "Y'all just ran right to her!" I said as I remembered how fast that clerk had moved when she walked in.

The clerk was beet red and rolled her eyes so hard I thought I might have to catch 'em. "Ma'am, that's *Anita Baker!*" She said just as snippy as she wanted to be.

Now in the safety of my mind I was like, *"Oooh shiiit, bitch, I'm shopping with Anita Baker!"* But I was teaching this clerk a lesson and fuck around and find out-nomics, and I had to keep my cool. Instead, I said, "Ma'am! Ma'am. I don't give a damn!" *The little clerk bitch spun like the exorcist as Anita and her crew walked out.* I couldn't help but laugh. Melanie put the icing on the cake shouting about how Anita couldn't do it like us anyway. The clerk looked torn, as if she wanted to run after Ms. Baker. *Shit. I wanted to run after her, too, but not more than I wanted what I came there for!*

. . .

The clerk turned back to us pissed all the way off. "Can you please use your indoor voice!" she hissed. "INDOOR VOICE!" Monica boomed ready to mush her ass. I looked at that last outburst trying to figure out if her ignorance was born of will or stupidity. *"Why are you talking to us like some damn children?"* I asked like Dru Hill, five steps from slapping sense into her ass. *That's when she started to backpedaling. Shit,* if the Lions'defensive backs would have had it like her, they would have won more games. *Maybe.* Finally, she asked the magic question, *"How can I help you?"* She knew damn well she wanted to be like..."*Get the fuck out!"* But see, that might have got her ass whooped.

With a polite smile, Mel and I told her what we wanted. "Ohhh, that's very expensive." the clerk said sadly, with a smile that said she couldn't wait for those words to leave her mouth. *"It's imported from France!"* The clerk continued like I didn't wipe my ass with what she made a year.

I told her I didn't ask all that, I knew damn well where it came from. Mel and Monica kindly let her know they saw the same shit getting boosted on Seven Mile. She tried to pretend that she didn't know what boosted meant. *Like white people don't steal!* Rather than argue the point, I told her I wanted the dress I picked out. She got cute with me again. "Oh I know for a fact we absolutely don't have that in your size."

. . .

I laughed at her silly ass. " Well, give me two then!" She looked at me as if I had sprouted a second head.

"Are you sure you want *two?* Just so you know, we don't *take checks!" The nerve of this heifer*, I thought to myself.

My friends just laughed. Her poor ignorant ass didn't have the slightest clue. I had this cute little fanny pack that I kept my spending money in. I began tossing money on the counter, "Take it out of that," a stack holding a few bands landed. "And that!" I tossed some more before spinning around and launching another over my shoulder. "And that." I said. Suddenly the bitch was all smiles as we brought out damn near the whole store.

Watching her entire demeanor change as soon as that money came out was a trip. Maybe some bread can't buy class, but you can pay for a little dignity. If I really wanted to flex, I would have took my money off the table and went to a different store. *I really wanted those Chanel dresses, though. That stupid lady didn't know a bitch was creative and that my cousin could sew. She stitched them dresses together, and I was serving it, honey!* Still the experience taught me something valuable. First, money won't ever trump being Black; it'll just buy you a little tolerance. Second, I learned I could get results, without being violent. That was best of all.

Six

ALL THE MONEY I was making couldn't buy the one thing that hindsight made me wish I could have. Time. I spent, but I also stacked. I had never forgotten my promise to Rodney to give him all the things that I never had growing up. I was convinced that if I hustled hard and provided things, I was being a good mother. Anything I would hear him talking about, I made sure I went out and got it, and my son stayed fresh. He loved baseball and I would go all out making sure my baby had the best equipment money could buy. I loved my son, and I was proud of him. I worked hard to give him the things he wanted while ignoring the thing he wanted and needed most.

God bless my mama, she tried to make me see it. Lord knows I had the best intentions; I didn't know that I was spending my focus in the wrong directions. One sunny afternoon, I was all set to watch my baby play baseball. I pulled up in my white BMW convertible with a black rag top, *excited y'all!*

I had packed my trunk with gifts from Rodney and a few bags of cash for my mother. As quiet as it was kept, I really appreciated my mom. She had told me back when I was pregnant that she would have my back with Rodney and never once did she falter. I didn't know that cleaning up my act would have been the best gift I could have given any of my family at that point. Instead, I filled up gift bags with cash and I couldn't wait to give my mom her gifts too.

When I got there, Rodney came running up excited that I had actually made it. He gave me the biggest hug, and it felt damn good. My mother, on the other hand, looked less than thrilled to see me. With a grin plastered to my face, I went to the truck heart swollen, and maybe a tad bit nervous.

If my head would have been in the right place, I would have known that Rodney didn't give a damn about what I had in my trunk. He was just happy to see me. To my son, the simple presence of his mother was a gift. I was moving too fast to see that though, and if I'm honest, at the time I didn't value myself enough to see it either.

"Mommy, mommy, I'm so glad you could make it to my game!" he cried, making my heart swell. I was glad I made it too. I always felt horrible for missing so many. I knew it was important to him, but that didn't mean I knew or understood the impact it had on his young mind.

Little boys need their mothers every bit as much as they need their father. As their mama you set the tone for how they are going to relate to and what they are going to expect and accept from women. I wasn't at a point to recognize any of this yet though. Instead, Kool-Aid smile still beaming, I said, "Look what mommy got for you! Presents!" I opened the trunk with a flourish.

My mother seen through all of it though. With a hard look at me, she told Rodney to hurry back to the field before the game.

My son looked up at me, "Mama, are you gonna watch me play?" I smiled at my son and said the only thing a mother could say, "Of course, I'm gonna watch your game." as if it was the most obvious thing in the world. Money I could make. Time not so much. The difference was money was always calling and time always seemed to be slipping away.

As soon as he was out of earshot, she started on me. "That boy don't need no more presents, Rhonda!" she snapped at me, her tone full of exasperated anger. She couldn't see that motherhood was an uphill battle for me at that point, and I was doing the best I could.

I looked at my mama trying not to let her tone or the look in her eye sting me. "Everybody needs presents mama!" I replied, "I even got some for you!" I said rediscovering my good mood as I handed her a cute little gift bag full of money.

She peeked inside and handed it back like it had been full of snakes instead. "I don't need it either!" she spat.

My mood deflated. I was out there in the streets trying to

get my son everything he wanted. I told her as much. She looked at me as if I was the worst shade of stupid.

"You just don't get it! Do you?" she spat.

"I'm doing the best I can! Can't you see that?" I pleaded with my pager going off the whole time. My mother tried to save the situation inviting me to watch the game with her. But the money was calling, and I had to go. The look of resigned disgust my mother gave me still burns me to this day. "I'll be back later; tell Rodney I love him," I shouted as I left. If I would have looked back, I would have seen my baby run to the gate, heartbroken as I left.

Neither of them could see my pain either. It was a struggle. It's not like there's a class or some type of handbook for motherhood in the streets. Neither gig offers sick days or time off, and only one has any true benefits. Neither one would fit in the parameters of a nine to five. There were moments I wished I could split myself in two -- one of me for the streets and one of me to be a mother. I didn't realize I had options. What I did realize is that it was strange to want him near me all the time, while knowing that being around me could be dangerous, making me scared to keep him too close. It's a feeling I wouldn't wish on any woman, to want to be a mother, but to be equally afraid of the role.

It's the moments like that, that I wish I'd had more wisdom. I wished I would've listened to my mother. I hadn't yet acquired the fortitude to be the mother I was meant to be. I can admit that now. I loved Rodney, but love wasn't enough to raise a child or be a mother. As I would discover with my other children, motherhood required a vulnerability that I was still growing. As much as I wanted to give it to Rodney at that time, it was like the old folks said. You can't get blood from a stone. Motherhood is as much a biological condition as it is a role and privilege. Nobody is born ready for it, and no paths of motherhood are the same for any two women. The only thing you can do is the best you can do. You play the hand you're dealt. The only thing you gotta make sure of is that you are playing to win.

If I would have just slowed down, maybe I would have saved myself some trouble. As my influence grew in the street, I began to become a target on law enforcements radar. I had begun to notice little things here and there. New cars in the neighborhood. People posted by my house where there never were before. Maybe if I had done a few more baseball games with Rodney and spent a little less time in the streets, I could have continued to get money in peace. I ran a pretty tight ship. I can't say I was scared, but the last thing I needed was them people in my business. One night, I saw this little sedan creeping around the neighborhood. It was driven by some chick, and she seemed way too interested in what was going on inside *my* house.

On this particular night, I was having me a little drink and decided since the bitch wanted to watch so bad, maybe she was thirsty and would like to come inside. I threw on my robe and waltzed out my door. Homegirl realized that I'd been watching her watching me. The way her face twisted up you would have thought I offended her.

. . .

"You watching so hard, why don't you have a drink with me!" I shouted boldly. "I got red wine!" I said, but she was already situating her shit to leave. "Oh, you don't like red?! I got white wine!" I shouted as she started her car. "Oooh, how about vodka! Oooh, ooh, or maybe rum, that's right you a rum girl!" I shouted after her, but she was already driving away. I walked back in my house to continue drinking alone. Sad part is, I would have actually sat and had a drink with the bitch. The Feds ain't the only ones that like to play games.

Even though I was out there clowning, I knew shit was serious. A little heat was normal. Pigs are always gonna try to eat; the key was keeping the heat low. But boss bitch that I am, keeping a low profile wasn't necessarily my natural habitat. In the male dominated world of the street, I was gonna stick out regardless. Many people underestimated me to their peril, and I'd hoped that law enforcement would do the same.

I should have known better. The hustle we had popping with the fake tax returns got us popped. No matter how smart you are or how tight or smooth your operation is, nobody is immune to snitching. *A bunch of people ratted.* It makes me sick to my stomach. All the people out here doing true evil in this world and ain't nobody telling. Delrhonda try to get a few coins and here they go running to the man. *Ain't that about a bitch?* I wasn't alone; Mel got caught up too.

. . .

Hearing the words, "The People of the United States versus Delrhonda Hood" did something to my mind. Not the People of the United States versus poverty. Not the People of the United States versus hunger, or child abuse. Not The People of the United States against injustice. No, The People of the United States versus Delrhonda Hood. An entire nation against me. I hadn't injured anything more than maybe a few greedy bitches and Uncle Sam's pride. Melanie and I just plead guilty. The government wanted the money back, but sadly, we had reinvested all of it in the economy. *Fuck 'em.* Luckily for us, we didn't have any priors. Because we plead out the Federal government didn't lock us up, we ended up with six months' probation, and these *fly* ankle bracelets. *I always did love jewelry.* I also gained a new understanding of the dynamics of how our government prosecuted and punished crime. Fact of the matter is, white people's crimes come with white people's sentences. *Let me have been caught slanging with a couple grams of rock though.*

After all that cleared up, I was back in my groove. I was out at the strip club with Monica and Mel. The ladies were fly and there was more ass in the room than a stadium. The ladies working the stage were getting it as the room throbbed with bass. We hit the scene young, Black, and bold. Fierce in the way only our generation could be. That was before clothes were made with Black women in mind. Drip wasn't ready made, and it for damn sure wasn't cut to fit with curve positivity in mind. *Working it* was a lot more work in those days. They should have violated Mel and I, just for how we slayed shit that night, and I'll never forget it because it was the night I met *Slim and got my name.*

• • •

47

I can remember leaning back against the bar, guns at a high salute. Guaranteeing attention. I had set my eye on this playa further down the bar. Everything about the man exuded competence and intellect. Like seeing a wolf among dogs. "Who's that? I'd asked?" Thinking about precisely how much I wanted to know. "He looks like he's getting money." From a chick like me, that was high praise. Plenty folk can be good-looking and ain't worth shit. But this brotha had that glow that said he was a man worth knowing.

Mel who knew every damn body replied, "Girl, that's Slim. Serious drug dealer, real killer, he don't play, and *definitely* not with women." She had just confirmed my instincts.

"We'll see about that..." was my only reply. I started flirting from across the room. I knew I had caught his eye and sure enough, he came my way.

"Whatchu doin' over here?" he questioned with just that right amount of bass in his voice. The nigga knew the game but so did I.

"Enough for you to come find out. Having fun, hustlin' just like you..." I told him letting him know he wasn't the only wolf in the room. Slim looked at me quizzically, a small smile playing about his lips. "*Hustlin'? Whatchu hustlin'?*"

· · ·

It was my turn to smile. "Don't worry about what I'm hustlin'. *Whatchu got?*" I challenged.

He spread his arms showing off a toned chest under his leather and said what niggas always say. "Baby I got everything!" It was smoothly done, but I still had to let his ass know it was the typical male response. He looked me right in my eyes and said, "Ain't nothing typical about me." Now, this again was a typical response, but there was a sincerity in his tone that let me know he wasn't cappin'. He introduced himself as Slim, and I told him they called me Chip. Slim looked at me seriously, "Seems like you got balls as big as your chest."

Flattered, I replied the only way I knew how, "I do! You betta *ask* about me!" I said unable to fight the start of a smile.

Slim pierced me with his dark stare again. " Oh I did." he said in a matter of fact tone.

For the first time, he had caught me off guard. "*Really?*"

I asked him, unable to completely cover my shock. "Yeah," Slim shot back without batting an eye. "I heard you like to do everything *big*. " From another nigga it might have been corny, but from Slim, it was a simple statement of fact. I followed his eyes as they traveled into that valley that men always seemed to get lost in. It wasn't a punk-asss quick glance but rather a nice slow walk down a hill.

"Why are you staring at my breasts?" I asked him just as boldly as he'd stared.

Slim favored me with a toothy schoolboy smile and gave the answer all men do. "Cuz they big." he said leering for emphasis. I rolled my eyes like I wasn't enjoying the attention. He asked me how big they were guessing thirty-eight, or forty-two.

I couldn't help but laugh. "Nah, try fifty." I told him. Slim's eyes got as big as plates as his eyebrows shot to his hairline.

"*Fifty!*" He said looking as though he'd choked on his tongue. The expression on his face was like he didn't know titties could even get that big, like he wouldn't believe it, but with the evidence thrust in his face like a five-course meal, he didn't have a choice.

Slim's eyes took on this sparkle when they met mine again. "I'm gonna call you, Big Fifty." he said. Little did he know that was the name that would ring out in the streets of Detroit for years to come.

. . .

I told Slim, "I don't care what you call me as long as you call me when it's time to get some money." Playing it all the way cool. Deep down I was excited.

Slim raised his glass and we toasted one another. He smiled and said, "Let's get this money then."

I knew then that would be the start of something. The attraction was more than a sexual thing. There was a fission of synergy. When we toasted to getting money, it was no idle mack. It was game recognize game, and in each other we saw a teammate. He knew things that I wanted to learn and had the keys to doors I wanted to open. More important than that, Slim had the aura of a winner. That added to a solid reputation as a street nigga was too much to pass up. That was the type of energy I wanted around me. More importantly, he had been running around long enough that he hadn't been caught up with no pest control issues. My little run in with the law had taught me a thing or three about *operational security*. Making moves with a playa of Slim's caliber was more than a good move. It would prove to be one of my best in the streets.

Seven

SLIM HAD a reputation for moving weight and for being fearless when it came to beef. What the streets didn't say, was that Slim was brilliant. Lots of people are capable and excellent at what they do. That doesn't mean they have the ability to pass those skills on. Slim had this way of meaning what he said and saying what he meant that made it easy to listen. As he became my mentor and partner, it was like getting to study under a master.

We didn't have Sun Tsu or the Thirteen Laws of Power. The only Prince we cared about bathed in the waters of Lake Minnetonka, and the only Machiavelli we knew about was the crazy Italian man with Hitler. I learned about these books later in life, and it only made me more impressed than my mentor. Through his intelligence and his experience, Slim managed to pick up these legendary lessons of leadership and power dynamics from survival in the streets. If there was a university for street shit, Slim would've been Suma Cum Laude.

I learned everything I could, and Slim taught me everything from the bottom up. So many times, coming up in the streets, the youngins and the newbies get exploited. I know guys out here that treat their people worse than Amazon does its warehouse people. Lucky for me, Slim was different. Unlike a lot of so-called *O.G.s and Big Homies,* Slim actually gave a shit about me -- even if he did tend to lecture on like a professor at times. But good looking out can only go as far as a hard head will allow it, as I would learn.

Early on when learning the dope game Slim was teaching me to weigh and cut heroin. He set up a triple beam balance scale and everything we needed to get to work. When he had another worker bring over a package and Slim handed me a pair of rubber medical gloves, I was confused. *I also knew full damn well them flimsy gloves wasn't cutting it with my nails.*

"What are these for?" I asked him.

He looked at me in that way he had and told me, "These are to protect you, from the white junk." he said seriously.

I rolled my eyes. "Please! I been around heroin before." *Who did this nigga think I was?* I remember thinking to myself. "I'm straight," I told him ready to start.

Slim looked at the work, then looked back at me. "No, you been around coke before. You ain't been around heroin. Heroin ain't cocaine. The gloves are to protect your skin..." He stopped, seeing me still poised to argue, and shook his head in exasperation. "I see you are one of those hardheaded people, who like to do things your own way. So, I'm gonna let you do that," he said as if he'd made up his mind as he put gloves on his own hands. Then as if nothing had happened, he started his lesson.

Returning to his Professor Slim mode once again, he began. "We are gonna do everything in threes," he said dividing heroin. "We don't do no crazy cuttin' in here, just add that, shake it up, lock it down." he explained meaning they kept the dope purer than most. Slim was about quality work as I'd find out soon enough.

He asked me if I had it and I told him "I got it!" Eager just to prove myself every bit as capable as he was.

Slim hit me with a nod, snatched up a few things. "Imma go move some work around, I'll be back." He said and left me to get to work and I started. Scoop, scoop, weigh, dab, scoop, bag. I had me a little system and a plan to get everything all bagged up before Slim came back. *I was good, this shit was easy, I didn't know what the fuck Slim was trippin' about.* Scoop, scoop, weigh, dab, scoop, bag. I was going. *I was good. I felt goood. This is easy.* Scoop, scoop, weigh, dab, scoop, bag. *Shit was going good. Why the hell did, this couch get so soft all of a sudden? I'm hot, is it hot, are you hot?* Scoop, scoop, weigh, dab, scoop, bag.

By the time Slim came back to check on me. I had bagged up quite a bit of work *and was fucked right up!* I was sweating harder than R. Kelly in Claire's just as Slim had predicted my hardheaded ass would be.

"How you looking?" he asked calmly. "See you got a lil sweat goin'."

I looked at him like he was crazy. "Its hot in here. But I got it. I got it." I said feeling odd as hell. *Didn't he know it was hot as shit. Nigga sitting there in a coat looking all cool and shit. Shit. I got it though.*

"Why don't we stop working for a bit." Slim said infuriatingly calm. I panicked.

"Why did I do it wrong?" suddenly afraid I had fucked up.

"No," he said, "You did it right. But you're about to O.D."

I looked at that fool like he was crazy. "*I promise! I did not snort any of this!*" I spat.

Calm as you please Slim told me, "No, but for the last hour you been touching it and absorbing it through your skin." He showed me his gloved hands. "Remember these?" I did, feeling totally fucked up now that Slim told me I was high. He tried to help me up, but as soon as he said something about taking me to the bathroom, I puked.

I tried to pull my shit together as he lectured me. He made sure to remind my ass that our first lesson was learning how to listen. The problem with lessons is, I really don't like to pay attention, and everybody knows that I'm stubborn. I apologized profusely. Sweating and spinning, everything I did was done profusely.

"I'm sorry. I'm sorry." I told him.

"I bet you are. Slim said annoyed. Whether from my know-it-all attitude, or the fact that I puked on his rug, at the time I couldn't tell. Looking back maybe he was mad that I had recklessly endangered myself solely for the sake of being hardheaded and doing things my way. It would've been a colossally stupid way to die.

A hard head leads to a soft ass. That's what they say and they ain't never lie. Some days it's a lesson that will never be fully learned. Many would be street superstars ended up strung out doing just what I did. Being high as Rick James on the space station had a way of punctuating Slim's point. As punishment for my transgression, Slim didn't cut me a lick of slack.

He pointed to a bag full of dope. "I got a bag of work that I need moved by the end of the day." He said looking at me as I fanned myself with some money. I knew he wasn't joking. He was disappointed, but I was too messed up to care. I was probably looking as bad as the hot mess I felt. As I lay there trying to calm my heaving stomach, with the scent of my own vomit sharp in my nostrils, he told me to get to work.

In that moment I could have seen him as cold or heartless. *A bitch felt like death and alien abduction. Keeping it real though,* I know that Slim was doing exactly what he promised to do. Rather than coddle me for my hardheaded behavior, he forced me to deal with the consequences. It showed me the kind of leader and man Slim was. It's lessons like that, that keep you alive in these streets. There's not room for weakness, there's no time-outs even in jail. Slim knew that the game meant walking the razor's edge across hell, trying to get to heaven. There's no margin for error. If he would have let me slide, he knew he would be encouraging habits that would see me dead or on jail. Instead, he told me not to come back until the work was gone. His tone left little room for sympathy and even less for argument. It was about more than getting money. It was about being successful.

* * *

What Slim didn't know was how fast I could move the product. His eyes about fell out of his head when I came back with the money. I knew I had upset Slim, and so I knew I had to show up and show out. I needed him to know that he wasn't wasting his time with me. I think that's what helped me graduate from student grasshopper into protegee.

Soon Slim was introducing me to all the movers and

shakers in Detroit. We would post up at the strip joint dripping hard with our pockets on extra fat. Slim would sit like some lord at his high table, holding court. As people came through the spot to pay homage to Slim, he made it a point to let them know who I was. It was dope to see him in his element. He was a gangsta but he made it look regal somehow. He enjoyed the attention, and respect, even the fear. I would be lying if I said I didn't too. To see the other killers' and dealers' faces dawn with recognition and then respect was addicting. In ways I hadn't even expected, Slim had helped me raise my pedigree in the streets. Maybe that's how I ended up with the father of my two youngest children.

Eight

SLIM STEPPING my weight up wasn't just good for my pockets, it was a sign of his trust as well. He was like that line from DMX, "there wasn't a thing about the shit he couldn't do or hadn't seen." With him behind me, I didn't think I could fail. Distribution just happened to be one of my specialties, and I had already impressed Slim with my ability to move work quickly. A lesser hustler might have found the increase intimidating, but I was excited to show off what I could really do. It's like Slim said. I liked to do everything big.

He told me that I would be running the show, and I was more than excited. I was about to order a round at the bar when I noticed what looked like the same bitch that had been looking all up in my house before I got caught up. Just seeing her face killed my vibe. I turned to Slim.

. . .

"Everywhere, everywhere I go, I see this bitch. First, she's at my house every time, every time I turn around, and now she's at the club too. This shit gets on my damn nerves," I confided in Slim, more than annoyed at this point.

Slim brought me back on track. "Don't sweat them. You don't want no type of problems with them people. Just focus on the work and let me handle that."

That was easier said than done because a bitch was feeling like Michael Jackson and Rockwell. The work though. That, I could attend to with no issues. Looking back, Slim's lessons about being smart and paying attention while keeping transaction times down were all his ways of trying to protect me from myself. I drew attention and I never shied away from it. Now in the streets, you might say this is a bad thing. I can admit, you might not be wrong. But who was flashier than Gotti, and y'all love him?

Slim's lessons were his way of allowing me to do me while being me. As a woman, he knew fear and respect would be more important for me than a man. As a woman, a low profile might have kept me off the radar of the law, while making me appear weak in the streets. Slim knew that fortune favored the bold. Maybe that's why he molded me in a way where my natural boldness would be an asset instead of a ticket to a cell or an early grave. Being fearless is a wonderful thing -- until it becomes your demise. Slim had been in the game long enough to know some things and used his experience to empower me rather than exploit me.

When Slim told me that he would handle my surveillance situation, I can admit it put my mind at ease. Most hustlers see you under investigation and get distant. But Slim was old school and looking out for your people was just what you did. I been in the game long enough to know that not everyone gets support like that. I was determined to make it happen with my work doubled. Slim told me to focus on it, and that's exactly what I did.

I found me a little out-the-way motel. You know the kind. The type when the cops ignore it unless they are there on their own time, and the owner give less than a fuck as long as you pay. The best part is everybody minded their own business. It was perfect for my operations. I knew that paying attention and situational awareness wasn't my strongest suit, so I set up in an environment that minimized that liability. Being on the second floor gave me an advantage along with the door and a

heavily shaded window that kept our activities from prying eyes. The peep hole let us keep out unwanted visitors, and the door was heavy enough that I didn't worry about some fool easily kicking it in. Looking back, there's a dozen little things I picked up that would allow me to do it a little better. There's so much technology now with drones and doorbell cameras and shit that I could only imagine what we could do with if we had that back then. I can tell you this though:, it for damn sure beat the shit out of hustlin' on some damn corner for the world to see. It was even better than working out of an apartment where the traffic would be noted and nosey ass people in every other unit.

Thanks to a stint in sex work, I knew some angles to the game these Brothas might never have come up with. It also opens up a different clientele. See, I knew about spots and where was low key. Motels like this might not be luxurious or even clean. I mean, shit, I would sleep in my car before I slept on them sheets, but what they lacked in accommodation they made up for in other ways. Knowing what I knew, I didn't have to be told spots usually had people in and out. It was all the better because they rented rooms by the hour. I used that to my full advantage. I ran my little shop in two stations, nothing convoluted or extravagant. Niggas make me sick with their bird calls and hand signs and flashing headlights, all that clever just to end up in jail anyway. Basic is always better, as long as you ain't being basic. Feel me? The game itself has never been complicated. It's pure capitalism and nothing is simpler than that. It's people and their bullshit that make it crazy. That's why I ran it the way I did. Slim had left me in charge, and I wasn't about to let this opportunity slip. That's why my shop was ran like it was, solid bricks out the door. Slim had taught me to be able to do it all, and I could have chopped it down. But fuck that! Honestly, that nickel and dime shit might work for some, but that wasn't how I liked to rock. Even after all this time, I still had a point to prove. Never underestimate a street bitch like me.

. . .

I had a table set up with my work, a scale, and space for my drink and shit. Then another for Monica by the door. Appointments were set by the hour, and I had my clientele in time slots like the Apple Store. A customer would come to the door., Monica would take a peek to confirm and let them in, and I would start the timer. Once the customer got inside, they would put their money on the table with my homegirl, Monica. Only after she had checked their money could they move forward to my station. Just like Slim told me, my clients weren't my friends. I didn't do much talking. I let them pick up their work, and then they had to bounce. In and out, before the timer could buzz.

I worked it like a nine to five. Staying in the spot meant I didn't spend a lot of my bread while I was grinding. The pile of cash went up; the stash of dope went down. It was a beautiful thing to see. The simple symmetry of the game soothed my soul, and if you ever been a hustla, you know that feeling of getting money. That yearning for the grind. If you're not careful it can take over your life and make you every bit as much of an addict as the ones you serve. Who is the real addict? Both dealer and junkie are both chasing a high. The difference is a drug you can go to rehab for. Habits can be kicked. But who can kick a money habit? There's no twelve steps twelve-step program for hustlers, but maybe there should be.

Meanwhile, my future baby daddy was working his ass off to get that spot. Even though I liked him, I wasn't just coming off the panties. He took time, he did things to make me feel special, and I enjoyed the attention. Just because I was in the streets getting money didn't mean I didn't need my ego stroked just like any other woman. Often times running the streets, the softness has to die in order to survive. I was always Big Fifty the Gangsta. To be honest, especially at that time, I loved the shit. That didn't change the fact that I was still Delrhonda, the woman. Rickey's courtship, and yes, courtship is what I will call it, spoke to something in me.

The man wasn't stingy either. He would put money in my hand and buy me flowers. Even though I had plenty of money of my own, I took it. I mean, who don't love money and flowers? One day he even showed up with a gorgeous fur. Keeping it real, I'm pretty sure that nigga stole it. Dirty little secret, though, in the frame of mind I was in, it was sexy and exciting thinking that he would steal for me. The first inkling was the glass I had to brush off the sleeve. Then the waitress coming to our table that night says, "That looks just like my fur!" It probably was, and it was like Rickey knew the way to my heart. When a man's willing to take from somebody to give to you, that's a man in love if I don't know what is. He could have approached the girl and tried to buy it. But where's the fun in that? It was bad, and that's exactly what made it good.

When we first met, Rickey told me that he would kill for me. That I was worth it. I can admit, feeling like he stole that coat brought to mind something the old folks used to say. If you'll lie, you'll cheat. If you'll cheat, you'll steal, and if you'd steal, then you'll kill. It made me wonder if it was more than mack from an expert playa. With a bit more wisdom under my belt, I know that there's good men and bad men. Ladies, yeah, a good man might do some bad things for you, but a bad one will too, and he won't bring you nothing good. Fellas, I will speak to you, too. Be ride or die for your woman; ain't a damn thing wrong with that. But don't die or go to jail behind a bitch that don't love your ass. It's a fine line between "ride or die" and being a simp. Remember who you make your kids with is going to be a part of your life, for the rest of your life. Make sure you pick one that makes your soul, and not just your inner demons, sing. Take from that what you will.

Slim was impressed with my progress. My operation had been running smoothly and the money was coming in. One night we were out, and he told me flat out. "The way you're moving that product is a thing of beauty." That was high praise coming from him and I'm not ashamed to say I basked in it a little.

"Oh, you see that, huh?" I asked him smiling.

"Oh, I see it," Slim murmured. "I see it all!" He took a look around the room as was his habit. "I want to propose an offer," he said pensively. "I want to take our business relationship to the next ..." his voice trailed off. I was surprised and pleased to hear what he was saying, but his quick change in demeanor put me on guard.

. . .

Slim got this look on his face, like a dog when it sees a cat. I half expected him to growl. His hawkish glare locked across the room, and he barked out, "Hey, Kutt. Kurt! Come here!" A dark-skinned brotha wearing a leather, skully, and shades inside looking like a clown came over.

"What's up, yo, you was short with my money last week!" Slim snapped, all traces of his earlier calm demeanor gone.

The nigga Kurt immediately set to hemming and hawing,. "Aww, man. Slim, that shit's impossible! That's bullshit! My money don't never come short!"

Slim cut him off, his temper steadily rising out of control. "The bag was light!" Slim snapped, anger evident in every word.

Kutt added insult to injury by raising his hand to Slim's face. "Man, you buggin'!" he spat, and Slim launched a vicious right hook that sent Kurt's glasses flying. Before he could fall, Slim reached out with his left hand and caught the front of Kutt's shirt.

Slim continued to rain punches down on Kurt's ass. "You don't play with my money!" Slim repeated, punctuating each strike.

. . .

The entire club had frozen to watch the spectacle unfold. The unfortunate stripper, whose stage Slim had happened to spill Kurt on, had wedged herself as far away as she could get. It was like the minute Slim had beaten Kurt sufficiently bloody, he came back to himself. He dropped his ruined opponent, and took in his shocked surroundings. "Dance!" he roared and as if on cue the club came back to life. That was the respect Slim commanded. I didn't feel the slightest bit sorry for Kurt. Playing with people's money is the easiest way to play with your life -- especially in Detroit where niggas could get downright grimy. A lot of gangstas might shoot somebody and the fact that Slim had used his hands was a statement. He had said the way I was moving the work was a thing of beauty, but so was Slim's right hook.

There's lessons there if you care to look. The first and foremost is, crossing Slim was a dangerous game. The second: don't argue with the plug in public. Maybe if he would have tried to make it right, maybe Slim wouldn't have whooped his ass like that. You could always make more money. It's always better to take a loss than to lose your life.

Slim came back over to our table, just as calm as can be. When he sat down there was no evidence of the violence from a moment before. Instead, Slim's crazy ass was smiling. "So," he said cheerfully, "I think we should be equal partners in the business," he finished happily. I couldn't help but to grin.

• • •

"Partners!" I exclaimed. "You mean like half, even split? Fifty-fifty?"

Slim's face suddenly turned serious. "No. No," he said gravely. My heart stopped for a second. Just before I could get hurt or mad, he said, "Nah, like Slim and Big Fifty!" he said grinning once more.

There was only one answer I could give, "Hell yeah. You think I'ma say, 'No'?" I told Slim. I was beyond excited.

We toasted our new partnership. I could tell that Slim was relieved I took his offer. I was a boss now and we were about to get that money!

Little did I know that my life was about to change in more ways than one. My grind was successful, my paper was right, and things with Rickey were going well. I guess you could say a little bit too well. Slim wasn't the only one cooking up a surprise; apparently, I was as well. It wasn't long after becoming full partners with Slim, that I found out I was pregnant. This time, however, I wasn't a scared little girl. First came my son Eric and then my baby girl Deja.

Every mother will tell you that every pregnancy is different. Every parent can attest to the fact that every child is different. When you have kids it's like being in a car, traveling different roads at the same time. One may be bumpy while the other smooth. One may have twists and turns, rotaries, and detours, where the other might be as straight as an arrow. The only constant is that you as a parent are in just one vehicle. It's your job to ride that road until the day you die because that's the gig. If you're lucky and you do it right, you have somebody that's gonna take that ride with you. Sometimes it's your partner or spouse. Other times it's your friends. It could even be your mama, grandmama, and often inebriated godmother. Whatever your village looks like, it's with the best of all hopes that you get your charges along their road as safely and incident free as possible. That doesn't mean it's going to be easy or that there aren't going to be speed bumps, detours, accidents, and emergency stops. The key is that you don't give up. Even if you fuck up. Especially, if you fuck up.

Parenthood is the one gig that you can't just quit, whether you work it or not. The world is filled with people whose parents quit on them. We see what happens. Especially in the hood, we see the collateral damage of what happens when misguided choices or bad decisions , meet selfishness. We see the cycles of self-destruction and chaos that creates. Children deserve to feel loved. Children deserve to feel safe, and no child asked to come here. Therefore, no child deserves to feel like a burden. Even if you fucked up, the only time it's too late, is the day you stop trying. I didn't learn any of that being a perfect mama.

. . .

When Eric and Deja were born, I was well aware of the mistakes I had made with Rodney. You can't mother from a comfort zone. I had learned that the hard way. I was too young and too scared to see it with my firstborn. I can admit that Rodney deserved better. I can also admit that if I had the tools available to know better, my I could have been the mother I wanted to be for Rodney. In those days I didn't understand how my childhood trauma trickled into all the aspects of my life. There was no Me Too movement. It would be years before I would learn that what had happened to me affected thousands of households like mine. Men and women both have suffered abuse and unwittingly perpetuate it. It's hard to see before it's too late. That's why the best advice I can give is to listen to the people that love you, and if you feel overwhelmed, ask for help. I will tell you this:, you have options that generations before you never had. Use them. I can't promise a magical fix to your problems, but what I can say is if you get a handle on your shit, it will make the parenting thing a hell of a lot easier and a lot more productive.

I may not have known all this then, but I did know that I didn't want history to repeat itself. Maybe that's why I went so hard. I can remember one year when I did Deja's birthday parties big. For those that don't know, it's a part of the culture in Detroit -- and in Black America at large -- for kids' parties to turn into adult parties. The music, the food, and the libations provided a welcome release, perfect for the cele-bratory atmosphere. Parties could go all day and all night. Why do you think y'all in your twenties and thirties can party so hard? The yard was filled with balloons, a bouncy house for the kids, a table groaning under the weight of the food, and another equally stacked with presents for the birthday girl. We even had a bar with a bartender.

Not only were parties a means of celebrating, but they were also a way to project your power and influence toon the community. A good party could get just as much mileage in the street as a good ass whooping or catching a body.

I can remember looking around and feeling like everything was coming together. I was able to give Eric and Deja the focus that I couldn't give Rodney who wasn't a little boy anymore. I spoiled all my kids rotten, but I had always given Rodney more things than time. It's a credit to my eldest son that I never had to force him to be a big brother to his younger siblings. Often times in our community children end up damaged and with damaged relationships because of the actions of their parents. I love all my children equally. That will never change the discrepancies in their upbringing and the time and effectiveness I was able to dedicate to motherhood. By rights, nobody could blame Rodney for resenting his younger siblings. He could have ignored them and allowed hurt to estrange him from his family. Too often that's what happens, and it warmed my heart that he was at his little sister's party.

Nine

THE EVENT HAD BEEN GOING
BEAUTIFULLY. I was in a good mood and feeling good.
I came across my homegirl K.K. who we called Little Bit. She
had a little drinking problem. Well, ok, a huge drinking
problem and a record as long as Grand River Avenue. She
had a hard time finding and keeping work, so I gave her a job
as a housekeeper and a nanny. I had caught her shaking her
ass and dancing to the music before slipping off and making
her way to the food. I couldn't resist fucking with her.
Drinking on the job was pretty much a given that she would
sneak a sip or two, but that ain't mean I wouldn't give her a
hard time about it.

"What are you doing!" I shouted after sneaking up
behind her.

"Ummm. I was just getting something to eat!" she
mumbled off guard. She and I knew damn well better.

"No, Bit, I pay you to work. You know good and damn
well I ain't paying you to party!" I shouted.

"I can't take five minutes to eat?" She whined dramatically.

"No," I told her, "especially not when you take a five-minute break to eat every other five minutes!" I stepped a little closer and caught the aroma of dank wafting off her tracksuit. "And you smell like weed!" I shouted slapping her arm. Fact is I did pay her ass. She could've at least waited till the kids she was supposed to be watching had went to bed.

Bit looked at me genuinely confused. "I do?"

I rolled my eyes, "Yes Bit, you do!" Sad part is she might have just forgot.

She shrugged emphatically. "Well, I ain't been smoking no weed." she said emphatically.

Now, if anything told you Bit's ass was a convict, it was the fact that she could dissemble like a champ and deny something to the bitter end. I decided to quit while I was ahead.

"Listen," Bit said eyes focused on the food she was heaping on her plate. "Gimme five minutes to eat this right here real quick and imma get back to work. Word to everything I love, I swear."

I knew Bit's ass was lying, but I wasn't willing to push it any further. I rolled my eyes. "Five minutes, Bit! Then your ass gets back to work!" I told her.

"Yeah, Yea, yeah!" Bit said nodding vigorously more concerned with her food than anything I was saying.

Ricky came over and wrapped me in one of his huge bear hugs from behind. Bit saw it, and knew he had just rescued her from my wrath.

"You know I appreciate you and everything you do for me." Bit said with sincerity only drunks can muster. I rolled my eyes but I knew it was true. She might have been fucked up most of the time, but she was loyal.

Bit sauntered away and Rickey saw Deja getting into something and ran off. I looked up and saw some shit no mother wants to see. My son Rodney had grown into a fine young man. Too fine for his own damn good if you ask me. My eye wandered past the bar and what did I see but Monica, my oldest friend, my ride-or-die homie and partner in crime, flirting with my son. Not the harmless flirting we ladies might sometimes do with a younger man. No. I'm talking about kee keein' and eye contact. The flirting you do when a man is about to get all the pussy. Now I ain't no prude, and although my sins may be many, you won't find cockblocking among them. But this was my son. His little ass should have been taught better. As for Monica, her ass definitely knew better, especially knowing full well what I did to people who crossed me.

She must have felt me staring daggers at her back because she came from the bar with a drink in hand for me. I took a moment to collect my thoughts. I wanted to fly into a rage, but I knew that wasn't the move. It just felt like the move because Monica was fuckin' with my first born. Part of me wanted to pick her up and toss her over the bar like we was on pro wrestling. It's not that Monica wasn't a friend who I loved. I wanted her to be happy, and she was important to me. She definitely deserved a good man -- as long as that man wasn't my son! Monica wasn't a bad person. She was just a ho, and my son deserved better. I decided I was nipping that shit in the bud right then and there. I took a sip of the drink Monica brought me and resisted the urge to throw it in her face. I don't know what kinky shit Monica was into, and it's not my business. But Rodney was supposed to be her nephew!

Somehow, I was able to calm myself to say, "I know he's more mature than a lot of the men running around out here, but he's still a kid!" I snarled. Monica started with the head movements that usually preceded excuses but I pressed on. "More importantly, he's my kid," I told her coldly. Monica hemmed and hawed looking everywhere but at my face as she told me it wasn't like that.

"Come on Chip, you know me!" she said, and that's exactly what I was worried about. I knew exactly what she was capable of, and I didn't want that for my son.

Instead of saying any of that, I said, "I know. That's why I'm telling you nicely. Consider this a warning!" I infused the words with all the venom I could. It was all I could do to avoid slapping Monica's ass.

"Warning! Chip, you trippin'!" she cried, actually looking hurt.

"A warning!" I said sharply.

Rodney noticed the commotion and came over. There was this defiant set to his face that I wasn't feeling at all. Already aggravated, the last thing I wanted to do was get into it with my firstborn.

"A warning about what?" Rodney asked so nonchalantly it pissed me off.

"Mind ya business, Rodney, this is an adult conversation!" I spat rolling my eyes. My son wasn't stupid, and neither was I. He knew exactly what was going on, and that's why he'd brought his ass over there. He gave me this smug look.

"Oh great! It's a good thing I'm an adult. So what we

talking about." My son wasn't as cute, slick, or grown as he thought he was.

I rolled my eyes, "Umm excuse me, but you are nineteen years old. You ain't grown yet. You are a teenager!" I reminded him harshly. Something about seeing Rodney and Monica triggered alarm bells in my brain. Perhaps losing my own innocence before my time and true to the desire I didn't know, I had to protect my son's. My first baby was no longer a baby and just because I had the proof standing in my face and flirting with my friends, didn't mean something I was ready to just accept. I could see that I had hurt him written plain as day on his face, but he chuckled at me.

"So, you think I haven't knocked off some of your friends already?" he asked in a tone that was definitely too big for his britches. I was still his mama, and it took everything I had not to slap the smug grin off his face. I hadn't been prepared to hear that.

Offended, mortified and maybe a little guilty, I lost my cool. "Little boy!" I barked. "You just swinging ya wee wee around to everybody! That's what it is?" I asked using anger to cover my shock and hurt. Rodney's eyes got cold and hard as if he was seeing me for the first time. He squared his shoulders and inclined his head.

"I'm not a boy; I'm a man, mama," Rodney said with more iron than I could appreciate. The look on his face alone was enough to hurt, but his next words cut me in a place where wounds had never healed.

"Sometimes I wonder if you even know me. But how could you?" he shot at me, showing just a sliver of the hurt and anger that I had always been afraid of. "You was always too busy doing you, you, right?"

Rodney's words hit me like a punch to the gut. Before I

knew what was happening I hauled back and slapped my son.

I would like to say that hitting my son hurt me more than it hurt him, but the look in his eyes spoke of a pain a simple physical blow could never create. There was fury in his eyes as he massaged his face. I wanted to apologize, but all that came out was, "Damn it, Rodney!"

He walked away without another word. The sad part was, I wasn't even angry at Rodney. The situation had me furious, but at the end of the day, I had hit my son out of hurt and fear. I knew I hadn't given Rodney what I felt like he needed. When I was in sex work, I came across more than my share of men with mommy issues, and to think that I had somehow harmed him on that level was bitter medicine. Looking back, if I could have handled it better, no man likes to be embarrassed in a crowd. I knew I hadn't handled the situation right, and I stood there for a moment frustrated and desperately trying to pull myself together.

I wondered how such a beautiful day could turn so ugly so fast. It was scary to think about the things that I had been missing that were going on right under my nose. I thought about the things my mom had never noticed about me coming up, the things she had missed. The thought filled me with a cold dread. I remember standing there just trying to breathe through it when Mel came by to check on me. I was so caught up, I barely noticed her.

"You okay?" she asked.

"What happened?" I asked coming out of my fog. I looked at Mel, but something wasn't right with my home-girl. She was dressed cute as always, but she looked off. Her eyes were right. Her gait and posture was all wrong. I had been serving long enough to know the tell-tale signs of a veteran customer.

"Are you okay?" she asked again. "I just saw you slap Rodney." Mel was genuinely concerned.

"Yeah," I murmured before I looked her in the face fully. I was almost as alarmed as I had been seeing Rodney with Monica. I told her to look at me, really taking the time to study her because I wanted to be sure. "Look at me!" I demanded before I studied her face further and it confirmed my suspicions. "Mel, are you hooked?" I asked barely keeping the shock in check.

Mel rolled her glassy, vacant eyes. " What?" Mel asked all shocked. "No! I'm just here celebrating my goddaughter and her birthday." She said evasively.

I wasn't buying it. Monica's bullshit hadn't flown, and neither would Mel's. I leaned right in her face. "Mel, I know you very well! If you're hooked, we need to get you some help!" Mel looked hurt but also very serious when she told me she was fine. She said it so sincerely I really wanted to believe her. She sniffled a bit and walked off sipping her drink.

The drama didn't end there. Rickey approached with my baby, Deja, just as Slim walked up bearing gifts. Just because Rickey and I were a thing, there was still no love lost between him and Slim. Despite being my partner, the two remained rivals and mortal enemies. I took the baby from Rickey who turned and approached Slim.

"Let's talk man to man for a second," Rickey said calmly, but his tone carried just the slightest hint of challenge. He looked at Slim as if daring him to say no. Slim inclined his head and they walked off a little way. Little did they know I could hear every word they said.

"Why you always coming around with little toys and shit, playing like you part of my family, bro?" Rickey asked genuinely annoyed. Slim smiled like a cat in the cream. It was his way to push buttons.

"Come on. Ain't nobody worried about you," Slim replied coolly.

Rickey shook his head exasperatedly. "You still salty about that Auburn deal, right?" he questioned, referencing their shared history.

Slim smiled and replied, "You done?" Rickey didn't like this at all. Even from where I stood, I could see him swell with anger.

"Listen, brotha, I'm just looking for a little respect here, brotha; that's all. Quit sliding over here. It's wild you calling my woman at two in the morning. What's that? Quit it!" Rickey spat.

Slim wasn't no punk, and he stepped up to Rickey like the obvious difference in size wasn't a thing.

"Or what?" Slim growled.

Rickey stepped a little closer. "You think you the only killa around here, Slim?" Rickey snarled.

Slim met Rickey's eyes. "I know I am," he said all iron in his voice.

"That's what you think!" Rickey shot back.

Slim smiled again, but it was nothing friendly. "Aint nobody scared of that little half a body you got on this side. You wanna dance?" Slim asked with a look in his eye that screamed for blood.

"Yeah, I wanna dance, nigga!" Rickey hissed. "Imma put ya ass on a t-shirt,." Rickey warned Slim.

"Make sure that shit one hundred percent cotton, my nigga!" Slim said with a smirk that begged for violence.

"Oh yeah!" shouted Rickey, but Slim wasn't intimidated. Slim was never intimidated by anyone.

He stepped close to Ricky, almost nose to nose, and told him quietly, "I want you to pull up on me, boy. You know my name." He turned to leave.

"That name gonna be on a shirt you keep fucking with me, nigga!" Rickey spat.

Funny how parties always come with drama, ain't it. It seemed like the party was a tipping point into a negative space in my life. From that day alone there's several things that if I would have had a crystal ball, I might have done differently. I know that I definitely wouldn't have went off on my son and maybe saved that slap for Mel. I should have dragged her ass to rehab then and there. Maybe all our lives would have turned out differently. At the time I was trying to wear a dozen hats while doing a hundred things multi-tasking my ass off. The people who study these things will tell you multi-tasking is inefficient. It sounds crazy, but it makes sense. When you're multi-tasking, you can't fully focus. You miss things or have to go back and fix things or they come back and bite you in the ass. Things like your best friend being strung out, and your son thinking he has to be the second coming of Wilt Chamberlain to get your attention.

I'm not gonna lie; it was nice being a boss, running the streets, and being a mother to my children. It gave the illusion of being in control. That's the thing about illusions. They aren't real. I was doing my thing, but as they say, when you're a jack of all trades, you're a master of none. Things were beginning to slide downhill. Law enforcement started pinching my inner circle over petty shit. Pigs call it applying pressure. If you get a slightly more racist breed, they might call it shaking the trees. If you ask me, that ain't police work. I call it law-based extortion with a dash of entrapment. No matter what you call it, they caught Melanie up shoplifting high as Bobby Brown in a skyscraper. After that, shit started to get sketchy. After ten years of grindin', suddenly the Feds had me in their sights.

It's funny because looking back I had so many gut feelings that I ignored or rationalized away. Trusting your intuition is always harder than people make it out to be. I can tell you from experience it's worth the effort. Like Slim said, I'm one of those hard-headed people that has to learn things my own way. Please don't be like me. Be as stubborn as you want to be with the world but check that shit when it comes to that little voice. That nagging little voice in the back of your head that matters when something ain't right. Listen to it, because it might just save your life or your freedom.

One night I was at home with Rickey hanging out and shooting pool. The phone rang, and I paused the game telling my man not to touch the table. Niggaz will cheat if you let 'em. I told him, "I'm watching you!" as I set my stick down and he picked it up. I made sure my back was against the wall so I could see his ass. I had expected it to be Monica or just one of those random calls we couldn't screen before caller ID and do not call lists. Instead, I picked up, "Hello?" A voice I hadn't heard in a long time came from the other side.

"Hey, Fifty, it's Avery..." came the voice.

"What's going on? I asked wondering why he was calling me.

"I got a friend that needs a ki and told him I knew where he could cop one." Alarm bells started ringing in my head

80

immediately. My gut was screaming at a bitch to hang up the phone.

"Rickey and I ain't heard from you in years and you calling my phone for something like this?" It smelled wrong even through the phone line.

"No, sorry, I can't help you." I told him. But then the nigga set to wheedling.

"Aww come on Fifty. You know Rickey don't fuck with me like that no more since we fell out. For me, please? " he begged. "For old times sake, I really need this." Avery's desperation sounded real enough. As a hustla, we all have them moments where chips are down and your back is against the wall. Anybody in the streets know what it's like to need that lifeline. So, I caved. I figured his ass was in some sort of trouble.

"Aiight, meet me tomorrow at the old spot." I said with a sigh. "Ohh thank you. Thank you!" Avery was saying but I was already hanging up.

Rickey had been half-listening. "Was that this nigga Slim?" I shook my head.

"No, it was Avery, wanting a kilo." Rickey looked puzzled.

"He tryin' to hop back in the game and hit you instead of me?" he asked.

"No, I think he probably owe somebody some bread," I told Rickey. "He said you don't rock with him and this could help him out." I finished.

Rickey didn't look happy. "I damn sure don't fuck with this nigga, and I don't trust him hitting you talking about a brick. Shit sound shady. I can't let you rock on that alone. I'm coming." he said seriously.

I was touched. Rickey always was the protective breed,

but I knew I didn't need protection from Avery. He was a pussycat, and I told Rickey he was harmless. "Trust me, I'll be fine!" I told him trying to assuage his fears.

He didn't look happy, but Rickey said, "Aiight I'm a let you do things your way, but if shit go left, imma handle it mine. You know how I feel about you." he said seriously.

"You gonna come to my rescue?" I asked teasing.

He smiled. "Look at ya, what else am I supposed to do?"

The following night I was at my old spot in the motel. It was just a quick drop so I was alone. When I heard the knock, I looked through the peep hole to confirm, then I let Avery into the room. He came in all smiles and tried to hug me.

"Back the fuck up and hold on!" I shouted as I noticed he wasn't alone. "Who the hell is this? No! No!" I said turning away about to get my gun and evict these fools.

"Relax, relax!" Avery shouted. "This is my boy Dade…"

I cut him off. "I got nothing to say!" I shouted back and turned to pack up my shit.

Avery forced his friend out the room. He turned his back on me to shut the door, and that was his mistake. He turned around and I was in his face with my gun.

"You know I should fucking kill you, right!" I shouted pointing the gun at his head.

"I'm sorry! That's just my boy Dade" he pleaded, "Please just let me get the stuff and go."

Against my better judgment, I gave him the work. "Where's my money!" I shouted ready to be done with the whole thing.

That's when Avery went to the door and called for the money. That's when Dade came in with the badge and gun. If not for my kids, I might have killed both them fools. That damn Rickey was right again. I was angry, mad at that fucking Avery, and mad at myself. In the streets, not all money is good money. I could have left that alone and I wish I had. I sat there staring at that white boy with his gun in my face and knew my ass was grass.

"Don't fucking move!" he shouted. I was too mad to do much but shake with rage. It's like they always say, "A hard head leads to a soft ass."

I learned the hard way that I needed to do a better job at listening. I hadn't listened to myself or the people with my best interests in mind. To make it worse, I ignored the lessons I had been taught. Let me break it down. My first mistake was when I didn't stick to my guns on the phone. I made it worse by being dismissive of Avery which helped me misread his desperation. It also lulled me into a false sense of security that helped me compound my mistakes by heading out there with nobody to cover my ass. I should have let Rickey come just like I should have hung up the phone. Chances are if Avery would have seen Rickey, he would have took Dade the pig and left. Sometimes it strikes me that if it would have been a robbery, my ass might be dead right now. My worst mistake in the entire situation was serving Avery's cooperative ass when I know I knew better. If you're out in these streets hustlin', and I hope you're not. Please trust your instincts and remember greed kills just as surely as a bullet. Its cousin, arrogance, is just as deadly. Combined, the two will end you, no matter how smart or how dangerous you might be. No matter how scared people are to cross you, nothing beats the cross but a double-cross. Remember that.

Ten

MY CASE of hardheaded and stupid landed me with thirty months in prison. I did my time and came home to my mama's house. As cool as it would be to say I hit the streets like I never left, that wasn't it. I came home not feeling right. Tired and sick. Jail is a nasty place, and I just figured it was a little bug I would shake. At that point I was just tryna live; the streets weren't even on my radar.

Maybe because I was actually sitting still, my mama was able to actually get a good look at me. I thank God that she did. Sometimes it's the people around us that see us more than we see ourselves. When we are stuck in our tunnel vision, we don't see much else but what we choose to focus on, but our loved ones are the ones watching us -- especially when we don't watch ourselves. One morning I walked in my mama's kitchen, hacking and coughing. My mama walked over immediately concerned.

"What's wrong Rhonda, you look pale." She said, eyes filled with worry.

I tried to wave her off. "I'm good, mama, just tired," I

told her truthfully...well maybe if we stretch the connotation or definition of fine. My mother didn't look convinced.

"What's that up above your eye?" she asked.

I had been wondering the same thing, but I wasn't about to say that. I told my mama what I told myself.

"I don't know, probably just a stye." I saw the change in my mother's posture.

"You need to go and get checked out, especially with that cough!" she said in a tone that brooked no argument. That didn't stop me though.

"Mama ain't no need to fuss over me, I'm fine, please," I told her coughing the entire time.

My mother shook her head at me. I was really too exhausted to argue. "You gotta take better care of yourself. Now, please, let me take you to the doctor. I looked at my mama and seen she wasn't taking no for an answer.

"Fine, we can go," I told her.

I'm glad I went. That knot wasn't a stye. Instead, it was a lesion caused by a disease known as sarcoidosis. You might be familiar with it as the illness that took comedy legend Bernie Mac and football superstar Reggie White from us. It's known to disproportionately affect African Americans, as eighty to ninety percent of cases in Caucasians tend to disappear over time. But for people of color, it tends to be more aggressive and requires more time to treat and recover. It's especially bad for Black women, and I am glad I let my mama drag me to the doctor's that day.

In the end, I needed to have a surgery and went to my mama's house to recuperate. As I got myself back together, I learned two valuable new things. First, maybe I should have told Rickey I was coming home a little sooner than he expected. Second, Bit is crazy as hell. Let me start by saying my homecoming wasn't what I expected. Now that's not to say I expect Rickey to be in the crib hosting quiet Bible study, but from the sounds emanating from the house as we pulled in the driveway, it sounded like a party was in full swing.

Lil Bit and I got out the car and headed inside. I almost didn't recognize my own damn house. I began to wonder where Rickey was in all this commotion because so far, I hadn't seen hide nor hair of him. Bit and I made our way to the living room. When we got there, it for damn sure wasn't Bible study. There were half-naked bitches dancing and some nigga I didn't even know with 'em. Eyes turned to us like we were the strangers though. Some leopard-printed heifer with a short cut jumped up off my couch talking about some," Hey! Y'all come to join the party?" Before I could blink, Bit had shoved her back on the couch with a firm warning to shut the fuck up.

Homegirl's ass climbed up her back as soon as it hit the couch. "What are you doing in my face? Who the hell are you?"

"Chill out, Bit," I said still trying to assess the situation. I might have done a little mental math to figure out how long homegirl was gonna get to keep her teeth.

"I am calm!" Bit shouted and I told her I would handle it. I sat on the couch next to the ho in the leopard print. I turned to her with a hello.

"What the fuck you mean 'Hello'?"

I took a calming breath, reminding myself that I wanted information and not this woman's blood all over my couch. "Who are you?" I asked her calmly.

"Why? Who you are?"

I can't lie, I chuckled a bit and told her it didn't matter.

The important thing was for me to learn what I wanted to know. I asked her who she had come there with.

For the first time, she started to look a bit uncertain, " My man. What's with all the questions?"

Bit was on her again, "Answer the question, ho!" Like we were good cop bad cop. I always thought I was the bad cop, but for the first time, I realized that maybe I had underestimated Bit's gangsta. Homegirl tried to protest but Bit mushed homegirl's little peanut head and asked her quite simply, "Watcha gonna do?"

As entertaining as it was to watch, Bit's antics were disrupting my fact-finding mission. I sent her to the kitchen to find a beer. I remember wondering if that's what was making her so evil, but it was obvious she was more ready to fight than talk. Once Bit was gone, I went back to task. When I asked homegirl who brought her there, she gave me the answer I was looking for.

"Rickey and this is his house, so Imma need you and that gutta chick to leave!"

Now listen. You know them multi-hit combos you see in the video games. I had myself a premonition of going upside her head just like that. But somehow, I kept it together. Maybe it's because I felt like shit, maybe it's because I knew that with the cat away the mice would play. Maybe it's 'cause I had my knife and thirty months of cut a bitch training. That didn't stop Bit from jumping on that ho like Batman. I managed to get Bit off and lead her away.

Rickey brought his ass around the corner oblivious to my arrival. He had some lines all cut up nice and neat on a glass tray taking 'bout some you ready. He was so caught up that he didn't realize that the leopard ho was tryna warn him. He sat on the couch with his back to me.

"Look behind you!" she finally snapped at him. Rickey turned and looked and leaped up off that couch like it had caught fire.

"Baby!" he shouted only for homegirl to echo him like some type of parrot.

Rickey tried to approach me but pulled up short when my blade snicked into the air hungry for blood.

"Shut the fuck up, Rickey!"

He backed off; hands raised in surrender as I turned to his new little friend. With my blade just inches from her shocked, terrified face, I continued my interrogation.

"You didn't see the pictures of me and the kids on the wall and realize he had a woman?" I asked with this bitch's doom in my tone.

"When I met him, he told me he was single!" she shouted back, lying through her teeth. Rickey might have been crazy but he ain't stupid.

"Now, I ain't say that!" I heard him boom with a chuckle. Even Bit interjected to say she was lying.

I ain't gonna sit here and say I didn't wanna carve up her face, but I stayed my hand. Perhaps for the first time in my life, I had an enemy dead to rights and in my grasp, and then I shocked the room. I got up off of homegirl and simply told her to get out. Bit couldn't believe I was letting her go and neither could I. A different version of myself would have turned that trick into Leatherface, but I was tired. I felt like shit, and I just wanted to get my life back on track.

When I think about Lorenda and Lori who had paid a high price for crossing me, I am reminded how lucky this chick was. She has no logical idea of how close she came to me etching my name in her face. I'm glad I didn't 'cause that would have for damn sure been another charge. Honestly, it felt good to let her go. Besides, I had a bigger fish to fry. Homegirl took off. Bit, being in a less forgiving mood, chased after her. I opted not to offer more than token resistance to stop her. Instead, my focus was on the man I had given children to.

"I'm dying, recuperating from my death bed, and this is what you do?" I asked him dangerously. He came and sat next to me from where he had been standing in the corner like a chastised child.

"What I do? I threw a party. I ain't sleep with that girl. I don't even know that girl," Rickey said with this pained look on his face. I didn't know whether he was sincere, still in shock, or constipated. I told his lying ass to get out of my face. He kept on with his excuses, and he made me scream at his dumb ass.

"That's crazy. I thought we was better than that," he muttered with the nerve to look hurt.

"What's crazy is the fact that you out here throwing parties and cheating while I'm sick!" I spat back at him. I will give Rickey this; he stuck to his guns.

"It was just a party! That's all, baby!" he said pouting as he stood to make his exit. "I love you," he said, hitting me with the puppy dog eyes. You know what they say, right? That line between love and hate is rrazor-thin.

"Fuck you, Rickey!" I screamed from the couch, and I meant that shit from the bottom of my heart.

I can admit that it stung my pride and my ego that the man I thought loved me was out partying with bitches. It hurt. He should have been beside himself with worry. It was rude and inconsiderate and made me feel like he didn't give a shit about me. I didn't understand why he would shit on all the work he had done to get me. At the time I didn't understand why he did it. I was as hurt and betrayed as I had ever felt in my life. It was like that pig putting his gun in my face after catching me red-handed, but worse. For a while, I didn't want to hear shit Rickey had to say.

Having raised a couple boys into manhood myself, I understand a few things. First thing is men are every bit as strange and mystifying as they claim women to be. The bottom line is we live in a world that makes little room for their emotions. We like our men to be tough and rugged and strong but thoughtful. He also needs that little streak that shows he's not made of stone, but only when it comes to us. It doesn't leave much room. That's part of why we have so many broken men in need of healing in our communities. It must be stressful. Watching the men around me has led me to understand that sometimes being a man leads to men handling stress in strange ways. A man might fill his life with a thousand distractions before he will allow himself to confront how he feels about some shit.

Rickey begged and pleaded and as hard as I tried, I let him back in. It's hard to know whether you're forgiving someone for being human and making a mistake or you're being a doormat for toxic behavior. Agonizing over that can lead to a cycle that leaves us needing to forgive ourselves just as much as the person who wronged us. One thing I learned is you can't micromanage pain. Life is life and like the Bhudda said, "Life is pain, and you will only hurt yourself more trying to avoid it." With that said, love who you love, and love them for them. Just remember they are just as human as you are and love them with the grace you would expect but take no shit. Look at Rocky. He got his ass whooped, but we don't remember those parts. Why? Because in relationships and in life, it's not your failures that define you but your comebacks. I say all that to say, for better or for worse I let Rickey back into my life. Yea, you read that right. My dumb ass took him back.

If I keep it real, I was unprepared for the changes that had occurred while I was out of the world. In that regard, jail and recovery are the same. Your ability to do what you want, how you want, when you want is severely limited. Take it from one who knows; take care of yourself because serious illness or injury is a sentence in and of itself. Just because your life is on pause doesn't mean that the world stops. Anyone that's been to jail knows better. The world keeps on spinning, and the worst part of it is there is nothing you can do to exert true influence or control in the world. By the time I got back to the world, I wasn't ready for how life passed me by.

It was bad enough catching up with friends and family seeing everyone and everything I missed. Seeing how much my children had grown and changed was another struggle. Then one day Rodney came by and put the nail in my coffin.

Don't get me wrong. I love my oldest son and I was happy to see him, but the fact he wasn't alone and the news he carried and who came in behind him -- that broke my heart. Rickey wasn't the only mouse to play while the cat was away. I had thought nothing could hurt me like Rickey's antics. They were bad, but my next surprise was worse. At first, I had greeted my firstborn son with a huge smile.

"Hey, mama, you're looking much better!" he cried with that smile I loved to see.

I smiled right back until I saw Monica darken my door behind him. As suddenly as the smile had graced my face, it faded. As soon as I saw Monica with my son, I didn't need much help to figure out what has been going on.

Deja had been sitting in my lap and I sent her to go play. "I get it. This is why it takes you two weeks to come see your mother," I snapped at him. Rodney looked pained.

"Oh, ma, it's not like that, I've just been busy."

I looked at them both pouring in every ounce of disdain I felt for what was obviously going on. Nobody had ever hipped me to the part of the game where your homegirl shacks up with your son. "I can see that, obviously," I snapped.

I looked around Rodney and pointed at Monica. "I guess you decided to ignore my warning!" Monica tried to make excuses like she accidentally ended up with my son inside her. People might make a lot of mistakes with sex, but there are very few accidents. I think what pissed me off most was when she said she didn't plan for it to happen. To me, it's just a stupid thing to say. Nobody plans for bullshit to happen. That's why you plan to avoid it. "You didn't plan for it not to happen either!" I railed at Monica who had the grace to look ashamed. My son being who he was tried to interject and come to her defense.

"Ma, it's not all on her."

I wasn't trying to hear it though. Monica and I had been rocking since grade school, and he was barely out of grade school, and I said that. But I was past words. With a well practiced flick my knife was out. I had warned Monica and she knew what time it was.

"Chip, you tripping," Monica cried as my noble fool of a son stepped up to protect her.

I ordered him to move, but instead of letting me and Monica handle our shit, he told me he couldn't because he was protecting his wife. Rodney's words were like a fist to the gut.

"Since when?" I asked, mortified.

My son hung his head, "Since Mother's Day," he replied.

I couldn't believe what they were saying. "You got married while I was in jail!" I asked in shock. For a wild moment I thought maybe Rodney was depressed and decided that suicide by pissing off his mother was the only way out. I wanted to kill his ass, bring him back and kill 'em again.

I remember the grip of that knife feeling good as shit in my hand. Like it was meant to be there. I really wanted my son to shut the fuck up and get out the way. I had business with his wife. Seeing as how she had been my friend longer than his ass has been alive, I felt like in the court of Big Fifty, Monica's ass belonged to me -- especially since she wanted to be a bitch daughter-in-law and shit. Monica was right about one thing: I was tripping! I had to be hallucinating, tripping balls in an alternate reality because I didn't want any of that shit to be real.

You ever been so mad it's either hurt somebody, break something, or fall out? I was contemplating a two-for-one ass whooping. I figured maybe if I dropped my knife, I could fake like I was gonna hug my son. I could snatch his ass up and use him to club some sense into Monica. A head as thick and hard as his had to be a good weapon. When you're pissed off like that, all sorts of violent thoughts feel rational. I might have tried it too. The same voice in my head that kept ranting about what kind of asshole gets married on Mother's Day without so much as calling his mother was pushing me to do it. But Rodney didn't stop talking. The words "Yes, ma, and she's having my baby," he said heavily.

I wanted to punch my son in the face. Instead, I settled for giving Monica a piece of my mind. "Being like family wasn't good enough? You had to become family?" I screamed. Monica's eyes welled with tears, but I didn't give a fuck. At the end of the day, she had been around Rodney since he was in diapers. This shit was sick to me.

"I know you ain't gonna believe me, Chip, but I love him!" she shouted.

I couldn't believe my ears. Bitch was supposed to love him. He was her damn godson! I barked out a harsh laugh because I knew Monica. "This ain't love; this is lust! You don't know how to love. You lust!" I screamed not just dealing back the hurt she dealt me but telling the simple truth. Rodney tried to console me, but I told him to take his pregnant wife and leave.

I don't care how much you love your friends. Nobody wants to see someone that helped them raise their children date their children. The fact that I knew Monica's track record didn't help. On the flip side, I felt guilty too. Part of me felt like I was responsible for his attraction to older women, underscored by a deep fear that he might be trying to replace the love he thought I never gave him. There had been plenty of moments in his life that were important to Rodney that I had missed. While it hurt, in his shoes I don't know if I would feel much different. It was easier to be angry than accept that though.

I'm not opposed to a little cougar or silver wolf action between consenting adults, but that was a dark day. I was as mad at Monica as I have ever been in all our years of friendship but it would pass.

Eleven

❧

IT WASN'T TOO long before I started rocking with
Monica again. Even though there was beef over her and
Rodney, I couldn't bring myself to cut her out my life. Until
it came to my son, she had always been reliable. When you've
been thick as thieves with a person since childhood, they
become a habit that's hard to kick.

Maybe that's why it felt like the most natural thing in the
world to be back in the whip with my girls. We were
smoking and drinking having ourselves a good time like we
used to. I was feeling better and getting readjusted finally
shaking loose of the last vestiges of jail.

We had been laughing and talking shit when Mel was
like, "Yo Fifty we should slide; this is where people been
getting robbed!"

"Why?" I asked her, "You scared?"

"Yea, we on the East Side; this where they rob people!
Yes, I am!" Mel snorted from the back seat.

Monica chimed in," Ok, Fifty, she do gotta point. They
be wildin' out here robbing folks."

I rolled my eyes and laughed. "They might rob other people but they ain't robbing Big Fifty!" I told them without a single shred of fear.

"Can we still lock the doors please?" Mel whined.

"I'm good in the hood, okay!" I muttered, taking the conversation back to where it had been going before Mel interrupted.

To be fair, the neighborhood was rough as hell, but I didn't give a shit because I ran it. Besides our homegirl, Lonnie, was a Detroit cop who always got us the best weed they seized in the city. If you gotta do some shit, it's always good to have a cop right in the thick of it with you. I swear if I didn't know any better, I would say Mel's ass was psychic. No sooner than Monica and I had gotten distracted by a couple cute dudes, two goons crept up on the car with guns drawn.

I caught the motion from the corner of my eye before I heard, "Let's go, bitch, run that jewelry, money, the purse, and that fancy fur! What the fuck you waiting for? Roll that window down!"

The nigga said it fast like an auctioneer. We all turned looking at the clowns like they was stupid. They had run up on the wrong fucking whip. The windows came down as the guns came up, and Lonnie bust the badge out on they ass. They weren't prepared for four armed women to draw on their asses like that. Even Mel who has been worried about just this sort of thing had her gun out and ready. Suddenly it looked like the stick-up men were the ones getting robbed.

"Oh, this must be some type of misunderstanding ladies," said the fast-talking robber. "Peace and blessing to y'all this night. Matter fact, don't you go to First Baptist?"

"Yea," Monica replied from behind her gun, "Amen and

hallelujah!" she snarled as the would-be robbers retreated faster than they had run up.

Next time I would talk to Lonnie it would be way less of a good time. I was home, taking shit to Rickey who was losing to his boy Bulldog, Lonnie's husband, in dominoes. I sat on his lap and took one look at the board.

"I got next!" I told Rickey 'cause he didn't know what the hell he was doing. The phone rang and I rose from my perch on my man's lap to get it.

"Hello," I said picking up the line.

"Fifty, it's Lonnie. Is my husband there?" she sounded upset.

"Yea, he's here. Is everything cool?" I asked.

"No, I need you to listen. DPD is about to raid your house! They called me wanting to know why my car is at your house. But that's 'cause Bulldog has it. You gotta get everything the fuck outta there 'cause they are trying to make a bust!" She said frantically.

No sooner than I got off the phone, the cops were busting through the door.

Rickey saw them pigs and went to work like some sort of ancient hero. He pretended to surrender, using the momentum to slap aside the muzzle of the first cop through the door. Rickey grabbed him and crushed him against the nearby wall. Punching aside the gun of another, he fired a devastating right hook. The cop dodged and took Rickey down with some ninja shit. He forced his gun to Rickey's head and made him like down on the ground. Another pig had charged in, shotgun leveled and subdued Lonnie's husband Bulldog. I just sat there. I was used to this shit by now. Even if it was annoying.

Looking back, I think about those times Rickey decided

he was going to go all Braveheart on the pigs, and it gives me chills. My children are lucky to still have their father. I can't lie and say it wasn't impressive to watch. There's something about seeing a Black man beat the hell out of armed pigs with his bare hands. That shit won't fly in this day and age. Let that have been now in 2022; them damn cops would have shot Rickey's crazy ass two hundred and twenty-two times. That's not to say that the pigs still didn't declare open season on Black lives, maybe the older generation just moved different.

They would raid my house what seemed like every other week. It was nerve-wracking, and I was afraid every time that something would go wrong, and somebody would get hurt. The thing was, Slim taught me the five and dime. Five steps ahead and ten steps to the side. They never could get shit on me. I even seen that nosey bitch who had been spying on me. She had the nerve to come and ask if I had that drink for her. I gestured to the table. A drink was about all they would get outta me. Slim wasn't so lucky, though. They caught him up on Federal charges. Since he was going away, he handed me his empire, and I was determined to rule it well. Slim had taught me the game, and I was gonna run that shit.

I tried to remember everything Slim taught me and the habits he instilled. Most things went smoothly, but my first solo trip to the community center didn't go so well for me. I made my way to Ms. Watts's office with a duffel bag full of money. My reception was very different than the one she gave Slim. When I walked in, she jumped up from her desk.

"Can I help you? she asked as though I had walked in to rob the joint.

"Ms. Watts, I'm Slim's...I mean, Ray's friend, Rhonda," I began but she cut me off.

"I remember," she said haughtily as I set the bags on her desk.

"I brought some things for you that maybe can help out here," I said feeling pleased with myself.

Ms. Watts peered into the bags and her entire face twisted up. "No! We don't need any of this! No thank you!" she spat.

I was confused. "I just walked through here, and you need it," I told her. Ms. Watts refused to be moved.

"No. I've heard about you, and we don't need any of your filthy money."

I didn't get it and I told her as much. I didn't see how my money was any different than Slim's.

"I know Ray and his heart," she told me.

"I have a good heart too, and Ray taught me everything I know!" I shot back.

"Ray is a good man, and I don't believe he taught you to be a hooker and a thief!" she said, her entire face twisted with hate and disgust. I couldn't believe the forest of shade she has decided to throw my way.

"I'm a Black woman in a game for men, doing the exact same thing Ray's been doing!" I said, hurt sharpening my anger. I opened my coat so she could get a good look. "A whore is all you see when you look at me?" I asked her daring her to meet my eye. I could see my words hit home, but she wouldn't relent.

"Please, take this and go," she said firmly.

I told her to have a nice day and took my bags and left.

The double standards had always pissed me off. It was no different in the streets than anywhere else. The fact that I couldn't get respect from my own sister cut me somewhere deep in my soul. I think people fail to realize that we are the same, everybody is human. Most of our circumstances are only separated by a little bit of luck. It's easy to judge people when your feet have never walked their road. Ms. Watts's behavior was worse than hypocritical; she had dismissed my entire life by summing me up in her ignorant box.

You see people use the word hoe or whore and think it only applies to sex work, and to each their own. But there's people out here selling their whole souls, trading in their principles and identities for a dollar. Just like there's people out here who slang a little ass. I know who I would rather have beside me when the chips are down and shit gets hot. Sex work may not be well respected or glamorous, but I know some hookers with the heart of a hero and plenty of people with so called respectable jobs without a lick of soul. None of that changed the fact that at the time Ms. Watts had hurt me and proved that your own people could be just as bad as an enemy. It can be a rude awakening to see yourself from another person's perspective -- especially if it's not favorable. From that point on, I made sure that I would take my respect.

Becoming a boss in my own right came with surprising benefits. Unlike in the corporate world, becoming CEO of my own illicit enterprise meant I had more free time -- not less. It also insulated me from the day-to-day operations. Like a queen on the chess board, I had all of the flexibility to make the moves I wanted, plus a layer of protection. I used my newfound free time to my best advantage and invested in my greatest assets. My children. Saturday mornings had developed into a ritual for my son, Eric, and I. I would take him to his favorite spot for his favorite pancakes. I would always tell him to slow down, but that boy had an appetite as large as his father's, and I could understand how Rickey ended up such a big guy. One Saturday Eric and I were doing our typical thing when this dude stormed in.

"Yo! You owe me money, Dre! What the fuck, nigga! How you in here eating, running around town buying clothes and new cars and shit...but you ain't pay me my money!" he screamed at a man sitting down eating his food.

I ignored them as did my son. Eric barely paused to breathe, let alone pay them any attention.

The man who was eating blew him off. "I told you Imma pay you, right? I got you!" he said.

The other dude wasn't trying to hear it though. "I need my money now!" he demanded.

"You see me here eating, don't you? Now I told you Imma pay you when I'm ready, Nick!"

The other man, Nick, didn't like this at all. "When you ready? When you ready?" he muttered like the words didn't quite make sense. Nick pulled out a gun and ordered people out of the restaurant. There were screams and a clatter as people suddenly decided they had better places to be and vacated the restaurant.

Dre, so tough a minute before, had a different tune now. "Aww, man! Nick, put the gun down. Let me call my cousin. Imma get you your money, man. I swear!"

If Nick gave a shit, I couldn't tell as he ordered the stragglers out of the restaurant.

"Y'all, too," he said to Eric and I who hadn't moved.

"Let's go," I told my son. He wasn't trying to hear it though.

"Mama, we ain't do nothing to that man. Why we gotta leave?" he whined, truly upset his meal was being interrupted.

"Listen to your mother!" the gunman shouted. "Take your plate and leave!"

After some urging, he finally got up slamming his fork into his food in a display of temper that I know he came by honestly. He grabbed his plate and turned to leave, eying the arguing men with pure murder in his heart before he stomped away. It would have been gangsta if he didn't have to come back ten seconds later for the syrup. We had barely cleared the door when the shots rang out. Eric didn't miss a stride or a bite.

I often wonder if there were more moments like that for Rodney and I, would our relationship be better? In truth, I was grateful for the time I got to spend with the kids. My bid and surgery helped me get my priorities in order. Even though I was the boss, it was family first, the streets second. After losing so much time and coming to within spitting distance of losing my life, that was how it had to be. See the game differently you up off the street level. They gave me clarity that I wish I had in my younger years. As good as it was being the boss, I still missed my friend and mentor, Slim.

It was 2002 and Slim had finally made it out the Feds. I was excited to pick my boy up, and I had a few surprises for him, too. When he jumped in the whip, he opened up the duffel bag I had given him.

"Damn, Fifty. you really bossed up out here!" he said looking in the bag like a kid on Christmas.

"I got four more just like that in the trunk!" I told him proudly. "Seriously though, things have really changed out here. You feel me," I remember saying.

Slim just smiled and shook his head. "The game is always gonna be the game. T here's winners," he said eying the money lovingly, "and there's losers."

In a way, he wasn't wrong, but he was missing my point. The old rules no longer meant anything like they did when we were starting out.

"These young dudes are different, Slim! They don't respect the hustle. They damn sure don't respect each other and they definitely don't give a shit about no O.G.s," I told him seriously.

I wanted Slim to be prepared for how the world had moved on without him. Too many brothas failed to make the adjustment and paid the price, and I didn't want Slim to be one of them. I could tell he didn't hear me though.

"I don't know about anybody else, but my name still ring in these streets."

He was dead serious, but what Slim didn't know was that reputation was everything and nothing at the same time. It was long after that night that Slim was out and about enjoying his freedom.

He was at the strip club one night availing himself of one of the stripper's attentions. In the door strolls Kurt, who Slim had beat the breaks off of a while back. Kurt walks over and snatches the girl dancing for Slim off the stage. Having sensed a problem, Slim stands up, ready for action.

With instincts still on jail time, Slim asked, " What the fuck is going on?" It was only then that Kurt would see who he was talking to.

"Oh shit, wassup, Slim, welcome home!" he said with false warmth.

"Yea I'm home!" Slim said without relaxing. Suddenly it dawned on Slim who he was talking to. "You tha nigga who brought me that light bag. I remember you," he said to Kurt.

"I don't remember shit about a light bag!" Kurt said. "I

just came to give you the heads up that this my girl you got dancing for you, so show some respect!"

Slim got this smug look on his face, "Oh, that's your girl? My bad. How about I send her back to you when she done?" Slim said airily. He reached in his pocket and threw a wad of cash in Kurt's face. "Why not go to the bar and enjoy yourself!" Slim said with a grin that told Kurt he could eat shit.

"You think it's a game, nigga! I'm tryna give you a pass!" Kurt screamed forcing his friends to snatch him up.

"How you gonna gimme suttin I been had, nigga?" Slim asked like he really wanted to know.

Kurt's friends dragged him away, but he promised Slim that he would see him. Slim had been handling clowns like Kurt far too long to be worried -- but maybe he should have been. When Slim was leaving the club that night, Kurt and one of his homies rolled up on him. Word on the streets Kurt flashed his heat at Slim. With his usual alacrity, Slim told him he had heat of his own. Needless to say, Slim was the only one that walked away from the encounter unscathed that night.

Slim was brought up right; he didn't believe in taking a life over petty shit. So instead of putting them in the dirt, he just wounded them little thugs. In his heart of hearts, Slim was a teacher and all he wanted to do was teach them boys a lesson in respect. But as they say, no good deed goes unpunished.

It was arrogant of Slim to leave them little fools alive. This was the second time Slim had Kurt's life dancing at his fingertips and let him live. In doing so, Slim had let his arrogance violate one of his own cardinal rules. If you're going to shoot someone, shoot to kill. In wounding them, Slim showed them boys he was something to fear, and fear is a mighty powerful motivator of people. The only problem is it's a sword that cuts both ways. The same fear that will have somebody too scared to cross you, might be the same fear that leaves somebody feeling like they got no choice but to kill you. If given the choice of having to spend my life looking over my shoulder, or simply killing somebody, I know what I would choose. Slim was a legend, but he was also the relic of a bygone era. My warnings about this new breed on the streets had fallen on deaf ears.

I don't have the words to tell you how sorry I am Slim didn't heed my warning. Two weeks later I got the news that would crush me. On a night that saw fourteen shootings and eleven homicides, Slim was killed. The body of a legend doesn't hit the ground without sending out shockwaves. Slim wasn't only a legend; he was a giant and his fall made the streets of Detroit rumble. It was around eleven at night and Slim had been at the corner of Ford and Six Mile. The news that night said that Raymond Scarelli Johnson, known as Slim, was responsible for over forty percent of the contraband on the streets of Detroit. So many hustlas talk about moving work. Slim moved so much work he made other niggas millionaires. The streets may never see his like again, and to this day I pour out a little liquor for my fallen homie.

It burns me something fierce to know that them same little assholes Slim had to forcibly educate came back for him. Rather than leave him breathing, they left him dead. It's like watching a movie where just at the moment of victory, the heroes fail, and the bad guys win. It's hard not to feel like an entire era died with Slim. Death before dishonor only works out in a world where honor matters. I admire my friend for sticking to his code and keeping it G until the bitter end. But I would rather have my friend. No matter how bad you are, ain't nobody out here badder than a bullet. We call it the game, but ain't nobody playing in the street. These fools out here will end you over a pack of gum and a hard stare. Being the hardest, the toughest, the realist is cool and all. The streets will sing your praises for it. Take it from one that knows, though. Adoration in the streets is short-lived, and it ain't got nothing compared to a long life. Notoriety means nothing to the dead.

Twelve

I WAS STILL RECOVERING from Slim's murder when I got my next big shock. I was home when I got a knock on my door. I was pleasantly surprised to see my eldest son darkening my doorstep. I hadn't seen much of Rodney lately.

"Hey mama," he said looking as hurt and broken as I had ever seen him.

"What's wrong?" I asked immediately concerned.

Rodney hung his head before meeting my eye again. "I filed papers this morning, I'm divorcing Monica," he said heavily. I can't say I was surprised but they were so in love, I hadn't expected it yet.

"Really? Why?" I asked, wondering if I had been right all along.

"Oh, just a number of things..." Rodney said protecting what was left of his pride.

"Let me guess, she was out fucking everyone?"

Rodney looked stricken. "Come on ma, too soon," he muttered.

I looked at my son, my heart going out to his hardheaded ass. *When people tell you the truth about people they love, you should listen.* I loved Monica like a sister, but she was who she was. I ain't saying you can't turn a hoe into a housewife. But some people just can't help themselves, and Monica was one of those people.

"Come on, Rodney, she was a whore!"

He pleaded with me to stop and I did. I could tell even though he was hurt he still had love for her ass. It was a feeling I could relate to. I had known their relationship had an expiration date from the start.

It was his next words that showed me the depths of my son's pain. "She got popped, Ma." Now that was a surprise.

"Damn," was all I could say.

"The Feds been on her; I think they want her to snitch," Rodney said.

"Nah, I know somebody been talking, the Feds wouldn't be on me like this if not, but not her. Monica may be a hoe, but she ain't a snitch!" I said with feeling.

Perhaps galvanized by my son's example, I had to kick Rickey's ass to the curb. I had never quite gotten over his escapades while I was down and out. Perhaps it was coming to terms with my friend's infidelity, that helped me see that despite it all Rickey wasn't going to change. He would pop by to see the kids. *Allegedly.* That was the excuse he gave anyway. I let him, because as long as no abuse is going on between the adults, adult beef should never affect the children. But that didn't mean I had to accept his behavior either.

One day I had let them *oh baby, baby please* get me caught up. Then as it happens, I caught him out. *Again.* Only this time I finally snapped. I might have went a little crazy on his ass. I remember him standing outside, clothes ripped and face all red from where I might or might not have been forced to exercise my wrath.

"First, you gonna put your hands on me; now you throwing my shit outside!" Rickey huffed, angry embarrassed, and hurt too. I loved Rickey like flowers love the rain. But enough was enough and too much was too much. He had to go.

Don't let anyone fool you into thinking that there's a perfect relationship out here. There's not. No matter who you are, if and how good y'all are. If you love each other, you are going to go through some shit together. I loved Rickey and I know he loved me. I'm not gonna lie; there was a time when I felt truly special. But relationships require more than love. People can be toxic as hell and literally love you to death. It's up to you to set and enforce your boundaries. People do foolish things when they're in love, so if they can't add respecting you to that list, then you don't need them.

With Rickey gone, protecting the house and my children became my responsibility alone. Just because you don't shit where you eat doesn't mean bullshit won't make its way to the crib. With Slim gone from this world, I had the whole operation on my shoulders. The fifty-fifty split I had enjoyed with Slim was now one hundred percent Fifty's. There was a lot of folk that didn't like how I was getting it. Maybe it was jealousy. Perhaps some of my male colleagues felt emasculated. Maybe they felt like with me out the way they could have my spot. *Shit,* maybe those bastards that killed Slim came for me out of fear I would come for them. Whatever the reason niggas constantly tried me.

More than once I had to let people know that Slim or no Slim, this queen would hold her throne. For many, Slim's absence was taken as invitation. It got to the point where it almost felt like I had a sixth sense for beef. I would hear a car come down the road, and something wouldn't sound right, so I would investigate. Once you live in a spot for a while you learn the normal sounds of your block. Cars passing by or headed for their driveway make a certain type of sound. Slim's lessons about knowing my surroundings and paying attention likely saved my life and the lives of my children.

One night I was checking my doors, locking down for the night. I saw a car come down the street, which by itself is no cause for alarm, but when I saw it had shut down its headlights, alarm bells began to ring. I killed my own lights and made sure I had *that thang* on me. I seen a nigga creep out the car, gun in hand, low and quiet like a ninja. *I let off on his ass 'cause I don't play that shit.* Anybody that know me will tell you I love me a gun. But shit like this is why.

I caught Mr. Ninja spinning his ass to squirt in the ditch in front of my house. I adjusted my aim and sent shots at the car, the muzzle flash lighting the night up as I pumped round after round into the car that has dared to pull up on *my shit.* "Wrong house! Right bitch!" I roared at my attackers pouring every bit of my fear and rage into each bullet I fired. "This my house where I keep fucking babies! I will kill you niggaz!" I roared from a place of fury that mothers of children in danger have discovered from time immemorial.

I might have done my dirt, but I never put nobody's minor children in danger. When that shit would go down, I would find myself asking questions. If I were a man would the same stupid games be played? I was far from the first woman to run shit in the streets. Madame Stephanie St. Clair had went toe to toe with Lucky Luciano and the mob. Odessa Madre was known as the Lady Al Capone that ran Washington DC. She turned to crime after graduating from a prestigious school only to be rejected by the Washington elite. She even ran a night club that hosted Count Basie and Nat King Cole when they were just rising stars. I wondered if those women had the same struggles I did. I realized that the same reason Ms. Watts saw me as nothing more than a hooker and a thief was the same reason I was constantly forced to defend myself. They didn't see my femininity as a weakness to be ignored. Instead, they saw my femininity and it made me a threat to be eliminated.

The fact that the streets came for me as hard and as regularly as the Feds taught me a few things. Chief among them is the fact that the *love* the hood might have for you ain't shit but an illusion at best and an oxymoron at worst. When you strip away all the romanticism, in the streets you either exploit or get exploited. It's a ruthless equation that leaves little room for sentiment. That's why the streets will never love you. It's like the arena of ancient Rome. You fight, struggle, and bleed for the entertainment and acclaim of people who don't give a damn about you. Just like Slim always said there's winners and losers, and when you lose you're less than nothing. Once you see that, you start to look at the streets in a

new light.

The extra static wasn't the only thing that had my perspective shifting. One evening I come in the kitchen to Eric and Deja arguing.

"No, she wouldn't! Ask her, I heard Deja screech at her brother.

"I will then!" I heard Eric shout back.

"Ask mama what? What's the problem?" I asked coming around the corner attempting to referee.

At first, I thought it was typical sibling beef until Eric said, " Mama they say you're killing your own people. Hurting your community with dope and stuff."

I can't even front. I was taken aback by his question. While I knew my occupation carried certain risks and connotations, I had never really paused to consider how else it might impact my kids. I had been involved in the street life so long, I sometimes forgot about the civilian world's sensibilities.

"Do you think I hurt people? " I asked my son.

"Not me!" Deja said before her brother could speak. "You're nice to everybody, and you give things away when people need clothes or money," she said.

I could tell my son was more torn. "I always made up different jobs for you, like a flight attendant, or a nurse -- even a music teacher. I don't know," Eric replied frustrated.

Deja rolled her eyes. "Everybody knows mama works at the post office because she has to deliver *packages,* right mom?"

I looked at my daughter careful, not liking her delivery at all. In that moment I realized my children were no longer babies and my actions didn't occur in some magical bubble. It's not like my kids were stupid either. I always knew sooner or later I would have to sit them down and explain some things about my life and our lifestyle. I always knew the day was coming, but as it does with most things involving children, it happened sooner than I expected. The time had come for the talk. I had wanted to protect my kids from the life as long as I could. The time to be real and level with them had come.

Often times we feel like hiding the truth is protecting our kids when really it just leaves them ignorant. But I wasn't ready to put things all on front street yet. Besides, I doubted I had to spell it out for them.

"I need you both to listen to me carefully," I said hoping I had their attention. "I do the things I *have to do*. To take care of y'all. That means the food y'all eat, the clothes y'all wear, and the roof over your heads. What I don't do is talk business with my kids," I told them seriously. The last thing I wanted was for them to follow in my footsteps. "But since Slim passed it got me thinking if something unfortunate was to happen to me..."

Eric cut me off, obviously uncomfortable. "Aint nobody tryna talk about that, Mama!" he said face filled with a swirl of fear and hurt. I kept on talking. "I need you both to know that I got money stashed for y'all. Including Rodney, and there's enough to cover my final expenses when the time comes," I finished.

My kids looked at me faces shocked and as sad as I'd ever seen them.

"I'm not saying I plan on leaving here tomorrow, but things happen. I plan to be here for a long time, but none of us can change God's plan. I just want everyone to be comfortable." I could tell they understood, rather than let them mope around the house I sent them to bed.

Deja didn't do as she was told. Instead, she lay in the living room curled up on the couch. I was upstairs in my bedroom, trying to decompress from my conversation with the kids. I half-heartedly plucked Bit's nerves as she tried to finish up for the night.

"Make sure you get that bathroom garbage too, Bit," I told her knowing she was trying to leave.

" I was supposed to punch out five minutes and thirty-two seconds ago," Bit protested.

"Well, that trash was there five minutes athirty-threeree seconds ago," I shot back.

That's when we heard the sound of banging at my front door. *Boom boom boom boom boom. Boom boom boom boom boom.* Only one breed of asshole knocks on doors like that. After so many raids it didn't take long for us to get ready. As soon as we registered what it was, we flew into action. Bit and I flushed whatever weed and other contraband down the toilet as the banging continued. *Boom boom boom boom boom.*

I didn't know at the time my daughter was on the couch. By the time I made it to the steps Deja was half asleep opening the door. "Deja no!" Bit and I screamed in unison, but it was too late. *Maybe I should have told the kids enough about the business to know not too open the damn door for the police.* The cops flooded in guns drawn. "Delrhonda Hood we have a warrant for your arrest!" The cop screamed as I was dragged to the ground. "Wait wait!" Bit screamed. I just work here I don't have nothing to do with this!" I couldn't believe how my homegirl had tried to act like she ain't know me. I only let her slide because she was high as shit, and besides Lil Bit didn't deserve to go down over something I'd done. If they took me I needed Bit at the house so my kids didn't get caught up.

The cop looked at me sternly. "Can we search your home?" the cop asked expectantly. *You see, shit like that is why people hate the police. They do little tricky shit like that to capitalize on the shock of the situation.*

What that punk-ass cop didn't know was that this raid shit had stopped rattling me a long time ago. Rather than spit in his face which is what I wanted to do, I told him no.

"You have a warrant for my arrest, not to search my home," I snapped realizing that if the pigs really had shit, he wouldn't have to ask me stupid questions.

"Well, if you sign this we can search your house and be out," the cop continued.

"What the fuck would I do that for?" I asked genuinely confused. It didn't matter; the cops searched my house anyway despite my protests.

Even though they violated my civil rights by tossing my house anyway, I did have some luck. The same lady that I had caught spying and offered the drink to had been watching me long enough to know that I was a mother above all else. She agreed to shield my kids from the situation, which was cool with me. I could deal with this shit, but my children were innocent and in no way deserving. I made sure to thank her for being cool, but Bit was back to her bullshit.

"Like I was just saying. I just work here and keep her kids sometimes. I don't even know her real name nor do I live here," she crowded jumping to her feet. The cops made her sit and promptly ignored her.

"Do you have any weapons on you?" the cop asked.

"No," I said wishing I could gesture to my nightgown and bathrobe. *I mean the fool has eyes. Cuffed behind my back like I was where was I hiding it, and how was I getting it?*

"Are there any weapons in the house?" he continued.

"No!" I said annoyed. They were searching my house. If them mothafuckas didn't find it, then it wasn't there.

"Is there anyone else in the house?"

Before I could answer, they dragged my son, Rodney, up

the stairs. My eldest wasn't all they found. The cop bust out two packs of dope.

"Supplying your son while teaching him to take up the family trade?" the cop asked being a smart ass.

"That's mine!" Rodney shouted. "My mom ain't even know about that!"

I tried to shut him up but he wouldn't listen. Next, the cop pulled out a gun that I claimed as my own after finding out it carried a two to five year sentence. Next, they pulled out some slick assault rife.

"Whose is this?" the cop asked.

"How much does it carry?" I asked again.

The cop smirked, "Twenty-five to life."

My eyebrows found a home near the top of my scalp. "Y'all planted that shit!" I shouted. *It was a pretty ass gun, though.*

By the time it was all said and done, Rodney was charged and given probation. They had more lasting designs for me, though. Once they got me downtown, they could barely wait to get me processed before they hustled me into the interrogation room. Once there, the officer who led the raid on my house had it all laid out like the movies. The big board with names, a manilla folder of photos, the whole nine yards. "I want you to focus and tell me if you recognize any of these faces," the cop began. He had obviously done his homework but not enough if he thought he was getting information outta me. Right smack dab in the center of it all was my face.

I peered at the board long and hard. Then I looked at the cop and said," Sorry, I don't know any of those people."

The cop let out a joyless laugh. "So, you don't even

recognize that woman right there?" he asked pointing at my picture in the center.

I looked at the cop and with a straight face, told him, "Never seen that lady before in my life." I felt like after that, the vein in his head seemed to compete with the one in his neck for which would stick out the farthest.

He kept his tone remarkably even, though. "We know you're not telling the truth because we got your phone records linking you to these people."

I didn't bat an eyelash.

"We got you with a gun. You get both state and federal charges on a weapon. Now, your other bid in West Virginia was in a nice soft federal facility. State is different. It's harder, tougher. Now, I can give you an easy five in the Fed, or you can do a hard two in state." This cop could have offered me six weeks all-inclusive on a private island. I still wasn't telling him shit. I might be a lot of things in my day, but never a snitch.

What most people don't understand is without the criminal informants, the pigs can't do their job. If nobody told for six months, you would be surprised how few people get busted by anything other than dumb luck.

"If you give us what we want," the cop said, "we can give you what you want."

I looked at the cop and told him, "I really want a nail file. You got a nail file?" That's when he got upset. If they weren't desperate, this cop wouldn't even have been sitting here talking to me.

"I don't get why you are protecting the people on this board; they don't give a shit about you!" he spat as his frustration boiled over. "How you think we got you?" he asked like I was stupid.

I studied the cop carefully. "You're cute for a pig," I told him, "but I'ma tell you this. From here on, I'm gonna go ahead and exercise my right to remain silent. I get a lawyer or suttin too, don't I?"

The cop shook his head, disgusted. "So fuckin' stupid," he grumbled enraged.

Cops never did and never will understand. No matter how much they try to tell you that snitching is to help you, it's a lie. The government isn't gonna come to you with a deal unless there are getting the better end of it. They will promise the world for your cooperation and forget they knew you the minute you're no longer useful. The streets don't forget, though. Once you're labeled as a snitch, it's like a stain that won't wash off no matter how hard you try. Before long, that stain becomes a target, and not just for you but anyone associated with you. If you know you know. Cops aren't here to protect you and won't ever keep you safe. There ain't a day on this earth that I would risk my family's safety snitching just to save my ass a little time.

How many times have we heard about people coming forward and being killed for it? Khalif Sistrunk was murdered in 2020 for the suspicion of snitching in Philadelphia, Pennsylvania. Chris Poole of Oxford, Mississippi was killed in 2015 for suspicion of being a snitch. You don't even have to tell; all it takes is the thought to end your life. I can gladly go to my grave knowing I ain't never told on a soul, but that don't mean that I didn't regret not taking that five years in the Feds.

Thirteen

ALTHOUGH PIGS LIE AS NATURALLY as they breathe, that cop didn't lie about one thing. State prison was a fucking nightmare. If you never been to jail, good. Just avoid that shit all together because it's nowhere anybody wants to be. Prison has a way of making you less than human. *Shit. At least an animal or a slave might have value, but a prisoner? Forget it.* In prison, you're reduced to a line number on a budget sheet. Your only value is as a bed filled and a tidy little check for hosting your incarceration. The prison strips away anything that makes you who you are, that you don't carry inside you. If you're not careful, your fellow prisoners will strip even your sanity away from you if let them.

State prison tends to be worse than the Feds for a number of reasons. First among them is they are almost always overcrowded, and your fellow inmates typically have committed more violent crimes. You're far more likely to rub elbows at chow with murderers, people with undiagnosed mental illness, and thieves serious about their stealing in state prison than you ever will in the Feds. To make it worse, state prisons aren't as well funded or staffed, making them less safe. When the guards aren't on their job, it increases your chances of having to get into some gangsta shit just to survive.

I had resolved to do my bid and come home. But jail is hard for a bitch like me. In the world, if people try you, you got options. Fighting someone in the free world is a lot less fraught [?] *fraught with what?* than it is in jail. In the streets you could whoop somebody's ass, and that could be the end of it. *But not in prison.* While inside a correctional facility, you're under near constant surveillance with the ever-present threat of getting time added to your sentence or being sent to the Dungeon which was the pet name for solitary confinement. Neither thing was something anyone would want. Often times getting away with an act of violence while locked up is a complicated process. Just simply whooping somebody's ass might require the exchange of several favors and even bribing a few guards. *Long story short, it could be a lot of fucking work!*

On the flip side, being non-violent about shit was just as bad. Something about being herded like animals and treated like children combined with crushing boredom makes adults behave like grown-ass third graders. If you let somebody slide, rather than take it as maturity or grace, it's almost always construed as a weakness. Let one bitch live, you get tried by a hundred. *With the closed nature of prisons, you can see how that's a problem.* Odd as it sounds, prison requires walking a middle path.

Too far left, you die or never get to breathe a free breath

again. Too far to the right and you're perceived weakness gets exploited becomes living proof you don't have to stop breathing to be dead. Who knows, maybe in some screwed-up kinda way that's the point. Right, wrong, or somewhere in the middle, prison forces you to find a way to deal. Maybe that's why they get to call it rehabilitation.

I didn't want to miss anymore time with my children than I had to. My plan was to keep my mouth shut and my head down. *But you know they say man plans and God laughs.* Just because I wasn't looking to start no trouble didn't mean trouble didn't just find its way to me. I may not have went to jail to be Big Fifty the gangsta, but in case you ain't figured it out yet, don't no punk run in my blood. There's only but so far from the bullshit you can stay when it comes for your head.

I heard about this book once called "The Crowd" by Gustav Lebon. In this book, he outlines the premise for groupthink and how intelligent individuals become increasingly less intelligent when put into groups. The larger the group, the worse the groupthink. This is why prison is full of cliques usually run by a charismatic asshole, a violent loudmouth, and the occasional sociopath. There's no doubt in my mind that's why things had to be how they were with Big Lucy.

You see, I might have done my violence, and I've roasted the shit out of my share of people. But I ain't never been a bully and never could abide a bully. So when Big Lucy seemed to make it her holy mission to make my life hell, it really cooked my damn grits. I was too used to running shit and handling beef to let anybody intimidate me. *That didn't stop that bitch from trying, though.*

I can remember one encounter where Lucy started talking her shit in Spanish when I was sitting in the hall minding my business.

"Whatcha staring at, Big Titty Fifty!" she shouted as she got up in my face -- or at least tried to.

I guess she thought she was tough with her little train of sycophants. I'm pretty sure she got her nickname from the size of her mouth, because there was nothing big about her. None of that stopped her from talking to everyone she came across like she could whoop them and their mama. I refused to back down.

"Listen, *Big* Lucy, back the fuck up out my face before I beat your little ass, her ass, her ass, and her ass!" I shouted calling out her and her cronies.

"Let's go!" Big Lucy shouted jumping in my face. I shoved her back.

Grown men ran up on my house with guns, *who the fuck was she*

. . .

"You might have all these other bitches shook, but you don't scare me! I ain't the fuckin one!" I told her knowing the only way to handle a bully was to stand up to her. As I suspected, she shot off her mouth, not hands.

"I'ma whoop your Black ass like you earned it," she shouted back. I stepped up close.

"I will have all you bitches on a stretcher!" I warned. I was ready to put in work on Lucy then and there but a guard came and threatened us with seg.

Big Lucy stayed on my ass trying to start shit. She never came alone, opting to always keep a few of her hench-hoes around. Anytime it looked like she would get her ass beat, she would make sure to draw the guards' attention. Like any bully, Big Lucy was a coward deep down. I didn't have time for it. I never understood what I did to her that made Lucy and her crew single me out. What I did know is I was past tired of her shit. One day I set it up so that I could catch Lucy alone in her cell.

Her bunkie left out, nodding to me to let me know she was there and alone. I slipped in through the partially closed cell door, ready to get blood on my blues. Lucy was sitting on her bed reading and looked surprised to see me.

. . .

"Sup, bitch, how much mouth you got now?" I shouted, throwing a *satisfying* left hook to Lucy's face. She took it well and lowered her shoulders to charge me into the bars of the cell door. It was a good plan, Lucy wanted me off my feet so she could get in the power position. What the bitch didn't know was she wasn't the only veteran scrapper in that particular box.

I used my elbows to rain blows on her back and the base of her neck. Lucy realizing that I would beat her ass into paralysis changed tactics, backing up and catching me with a smooth right hand. Pissed off she hit me, I kicked that bitch in the chest as hard as I could launching her back across the cell. After that, I didn't let her recover. I grabbed Lucy by the throat and used her head to hit every hard surface I could find. If I would've known what I know now, I would have left her ass dangling from the top bunk by a sheet. After that, I had to fight Lucy and her cronies every day till they sent me to seg.

Movies and T.V. has people thinking they understand solitary. *You don't.* Not unless you been there. *You ever sit in the darkness of a fully lit room?* Won't nothing in this world bring you face to face with your demons like isolation. There's a reason even the fearless fear solitary. It's a trial on the mind, body and spirit. The human soul was never meant for solitary isolation. Seg is a monster, a lurking demon of pure malevolence that preys on your sanity with infinite patience. Hour by hour, day by day, it strips a bite here, and a bite there. That's why some people can go into seg and never come out the same again. Not only does it eat at your mind and spirit, or maybe perhaps because it does, it takes a toll on your body as well. That spiritual oppression is why I think lots of people get sick in jail, and with my pre-existing condition, it was rough.

The prison doctors really didn't know how to deal with my sarcoidosis. It took them weeks to come up with a plan, and during that time, I suffered. I couldn't eat, and I couldn't stand the idea of my medicine, so refused to take it. I missed my children, but it was deeper than that. Maybe it was seg. Maybe it was Slim dying and ending my romantic relationship with Rickey. Maybe it was all the negative energy from Lucy and her hatin' ass cronies. *Shit, it might have been all that put together.* But whatever the cause, I was seriously depressed.

Our prison system isn't designed to help people, so you can only imagine how effective it is at treating mental health issues. In most prisons the answer is restraints, and turning people into zombies with medication. You would think the system would be pro-therapy over pro-drugs, but as a whole, it's not. *Jail is a depressing place.* Shit, even the guards are depressed. To my mind that should mean mental health should be every prison's top priority. But prisons make too much money off crime to start making sure inmates leave their doors better people.

As for me, at that time it wouldn't have mattered what they did. *They could have sent me Dr. Ish, and Iyanla, and I wouldn't have said a mumbling word to 'em.*

. . .

I was tired. It felt like I had been fighting uphill all my life, and I was over it. All my hustle, ambition, and hard work had amounted to me laying in that hospital infirmary. *What was the point in any of it?* I think for the first time ever I began to question the life I chose with true disillusionment. If you've ever been depressed before, you know the drill with the spiral. *Starting with the what if's like Disney + and shit.* Until finally you twist and wind down the line of your thoughts until you arrive at your personal sunken place where you've hypnotized yourself into thinking you're less than you are.

When you get depressed in the free world, you can change your environment, change your vibe. You have friends and family you can surround yourself with. You can go for a walk. Take a road trip. You can find a quiet place. Shit, *you can go shopping.* Good luck doing any of that in prison. *Especially the quiet space.* For me, I think my depression at that time was part of a greater growth process.

Jail is boring. That's exactly how you want it to be, because if shit's exciting...it's usually not good. So I lay in the bed, bored to literal tears. There was no television and the only thing there for me to read was an old Bible. Honestly, I had never read it before. I had never stopped my grind to pull up at church on Sundays. Like so many things, church and the Bible were things I didn't have time for. Maybe that's why I had been brought to that exact moment in my life where it was just me, my God and that Bible. No where to go, nowhere to be, no distractions. I picked the Bible up and I started reading.

I can't lie the first verse I came across scared the shit out of me. Hebrews 10:26

"For if we go on sinning deliberately after receiving the knowledge of the truth, there no longer remains a sacrifice for sins,"

Seeing that made my heart climb up high in my throat. I knew that I had done things that required the Lord's forgiveness. To think that I had fucked it up left me terrified. The monitor that was tracking my heart began to beep faster. I almost stopped, but something kept me going. I was glad I kept reading. As I thumbed through the pages, I soaked in the words, and I let God speak to me. I passed First Corinthians 15:33.

Do not be deceived: "Bad company corrupts good character."
Something about that brought me peace. I can see God's guiding hand now and how He helped me open my heart to His love. It was there for me the entire time, but until you open yourself up and accept it, then God's love can't fulfill its purpose. Like the song said, "twas been blind but now I see."

That day I prayed like I had never prayed in my life. I begged Him to spare my life and give me the time I needed to watch my children grow. With a humble heart, I repented before the Lord and He heard my cry. I would like to say the whole prison broke out into "Oh Happy Day" like in "Sister Act", but it ain't go down like that. Instead, my soul sang and that was good enough for me. Like the scales fell from the eyes of Saul, so too did the weights fall off my heart.

I finished my bid and made it home to my family. I was having lunch with my mother one afternoon when she looked at me and said, "Sometimes I blame myself for you ending up in prison." I turned and looked at my mother shocked.

"Ma! I'm a grown woman; my choices were just that, my choices." But that's not what my mother meant. When I looked at my mother I saw hurt in her eyes.

"As a child, you were always happy. Always with a smile like sunshine. My little Chocolate Chip." Tears welled in my mother's eyes. "I should have known something was wrong when that smile stopped." My mama is a tough lady, and when she began to break down, my heart broke with hers. "I should have known that such anger and rage didn't just come from thin air. I should have known that *something* was wrong. It was my job as a mother to know!" she said with a sob.

I realized what my mother was talking about. I will never forget what my uncle did after luring me into the basement that day. Maybe one of these days I'll write to y'all again and talk about it a little more.

My mother apologized to me for being unable to stop the abuse, or notice it had happened. I had never sought or expected such an apology. I never thought it was necessary. But as a mother, I understood all too well why she needed to apologize to me. So I accepted her apology. I had been around long enough to know that when you love your children, the last thing you ever want is to feel is like you've been negligent when you did your best. I know that my mother would have protected me if given the opportunity. She's shot at people for far less. What I didn't know is I needed to hear her say those words just as much as my mama needed to get them off her chest.

It was a powerful moment in my life. A healing moment. My mother spoke to a pain that I had left unaddressed for so long. The truth is my mama saw what I hadn't seen. She saw how the abuse had changed my personality and guided my actions and reactions well into adulthood. My mama held me and we cried together, shedding years of pain and estrangement.

Scars and survival are things that come hand in hand. Nobody comes through life untouched. The problems come because we don't treat the wounds to our spirit the same way we handle the wounds to our flesh. If you get a cut, the first thing you do is clean it out, removing all the trash before you cover it with a clean bandage. After a while of being covered, you remove it to let the air help complete the healing process. It may be tender but eventually a scab forms and it heals. The best part is if you do what you're supposed to do, the scar will only be a faint echo of the injury. We don't take these same steps with our spiritual or emotional injuries. Often times we don't clean things out and leave the trash inside to fester. Or we cover it up and wrap it so tightly that we suffocate any new growth and healing. Eventually if left unattended, it will poison you. That's exactly why for many of us our greatest enemy will always be ourselves.

With this event I once again see God working in my life. My mother's surprise apology had charged my spiritual growth, and it's a good thing, too. It turns out that I wasn't the only one with some unhealed trauma in my family. I had made plans with Rodney to meet up and get to meet my grandchildren. I was excited and grateful because, frankly, our relationship had been a lot rockier than I would have liked.

When he let me in, I let him know that I appreciated him for letting me come by and told him I was proud of him for starting over. I'm not quite sure what I was expecting, but skepticism wasn't on my list.

"Really?" Rodney asked like I had told him I was going to join the circus on the moon. I was shocked.

"Of course, why wouldn't I be?" I asked totally blindsided. I may not have been as present as either of us would have preferred, but my son was still my first love.

. . .

"Ma, you're talking to the kid you wanted to *abort*," Rodney told me, and I realized looking at his face that he and I needed to talk.

Monica was late bringing the kids which gave us some time. We sat down and I gave my eldest child the real.

"I was fifteen, having a kid didn't even make sense because I was still a kid. I was scared. But I didn't abort you. I had you and I loved you from the minute you got here," I told him willing him to understand the truth of my heart. Sadly, it wasn't enough to cut through his hurt.

"I bet you didn't know that I was *really* good at baseball. But how could you when you were never at a game?"

I tried to give Rodney all the same excuses I gave myself. "*I had to work, I had to make money to support you, I was doing the best I could, but I can't be two places at once. Just because I couldn't always be there when you wanted me too didn't mean that I didn't love you.*"

While I meant every word, in the face of my son's pain I saw them for what they were. Hollow. Once again I saw the hand of God moving in my life. Up until that point I hadn't seen nor had I understood Rodney's pain.

. . .

My son looked with sadness deep in his eyes. "I'm not one of your clients you can buy off, Mama; you can't buy love. You spent no time with me! I'm just glad Eric and Deja didn't have it like I did!" The raw pain in his voice broke my heart. I remembered my words to my mother all those years ago. Mama was right. He didn't need or want presents. Rodney wanted his mother.

"You never wanted for anything," I tried to tell him.

Rodney looked at me. "Mama, I'm grateful for the materialistic things, but all I really wanted was my mother." Hearing my own insecurities echoed from my son's lips as the truth took the wind out of any resistance I had. Rodney was right. I truly wished that I could turn back time and change it, but with that being impossible I did the next best thing. I made the best use of the time I had left. It served as reinforcement for things to come.

Just because I had left the street alone, don't mean the streets left me alone. Once you rip and run the streets for so long, the shit gets in your blood. Temptation was always in my face. No matter how many times somebody would pull up with a scheme and a plan to get this money, the streets would sing my name like a lost lover's. Once I even jumped in the car, ready to ride back to my old life. But something about the way my kids stared at me from the front porch tore at my soul. I didn't even make it to the end of the block before I had my homie let me out. I went back to my kids. Something about the way they wrapped their arms around me, happy to see me even though I hadn't been gone five minutes, reminded me of what was truly important in this life. Money, power, and respect are cool, but what does any of that mean without love?

Epilogue

I HOPE that everyone who reads this finds value. Maybe you can avoid some of the mistakes that I've made and learn from my pain. We see the American Gangsters, the Trap Queens, and things like that and forget that the streets are a dangerous place that will take your life or destroy it. I know how easy it is to be seduced. There's not a day that goes by that I don't think about how blessed I am. Not many can get to where I was in the game without leaving in a box or in witness protection. I did my time ten toes down and never snitched, rose to the top, and walked away. Not because I was forced to, but because I literally had better shit to do. I think there's power in that. There's not many people who get to retire from the game on their own terms.

Now, I'm not saying I did it the best, and I damn sure don't want you to follow in my footsteps. But I do hope you think about your life, think about your actions, and the things that motivate you. If you don't like what you see, then change it.

If you don't like the game, stop playing. The trap is only a trap as long as you take the bait. Now I know that's harder than it sounds, but I promise you it doesn't take superpowers; all it takes is willpower and the desire to get it done. Take it from one who knows. There ain't nothing more gangsta than that.

About Big Fifty

Delrhonda Denise Hood was born on October 28th to parents, Joann and Willi Hood Sr., as the eldest of four siblings. She was raised on the east side of Detroit, Michigan where she attended public school. Delrhonda grew up as a very fashionable child who loved nice clothes and nice shoes. In fact, her father customarily bought her new shoes every Friday, so her innocent mind determined that the previous pair had to be thrown away. That notion, however, was handily dispelled once her mother discovered all her shoes in the trash. Nonetheless, that didn't stop her from trying to show off her shoes to the boys at school. When she was five years old, she loudly and continuously patted her feet on the floor to capture one particular boy's attention. Despite her persistent and best efforts when he didn't respond to her advances, she clocked him in the head with one of the wooden classroom chairs.

As she advanced through elementary school, so too did her body, and much faster than the other fourth graders in her school. She had beautiful long eyelashes, thick eyebrows, and, yes you guessed it, shapely breasts. She often wondered why the teachers would say she was a "fast ass" because of these features. As a result of being teased by the other children, ridiculed by adults, and even taunted by school teachers, she became more self-conscious about her developed attributes. Growing up in a house full of aunts and uncles, she always felt more mature and more intelligent than the other children her same age. Feeling that they were just too immature for her, she spent most of her time with the adults around her.

By the time Delrhonda was 15, she found herself pregnant with her first child, Rodney. She never really knew what it meant to be a child herself; she was a mother. At 18, a taste of the unforgiving streets of Detroit hastened her hanging out and becoming very close with one of the dancers at the local strip club where, quickly, Delrhonda realized her shapely and blossomed physique could make fast, easy money. So, that's exactly what she and her friend did. Even her neighbors recognized the same red limousine pulling up every Thursday when Delrhonda and her friend would enter it, remain a short time, and exit $2,500 richer. As she got older, her thirst intensified for the quick money and fast life of the drug and gang-filled neighborhood in which she lived. The decision that resulted from this enticement proved to be one she would never forget. This decision created "Big Fifty", the self-proclaimed Queen Scorpio, the Baddest Female Gangster in Detroit. She hung out with the male gangsters, drug dealers, and hustlers and took the Detroit drug game to the next level where business was booming, and the money was flowing. Money was so plentiful that she pampered herself with the finer things in life. She had the respect of the street, and nobody dared to cross her. She had the streets on lock. Having had two more children, Eric and Deja, during this time, she tried valiantly to shelter and keep them from the street life she was living.

Millions of dollars later, Delrhonda soon realized that this life was not all glitz and glamour, especially when after being set up, she served time in prison. Delrhonda's health began to deteriorate, and she was diagnosed with a condition she still deals with to this day, sarcoidosis, a chronic illness that causes several medical complications.

Today, Delrhonda "Big Fifty" Hood, is still killing the game, but on a totally different level! While still dreaming big, she has turned her past experiences into passion and purpose, and it's evident through all her endeavors. She's a successful business owner with her own line of feminine products and the host of a popular radio show called "Keeping it 100 With Big Fifty" where she uses her powerful, raspy voice to keep it honest and real while allowing her audience to call in for first hand advice on personal issues. In addition, she's also a recording artist whose hit single, "Do It Like Big Fifty", is bumpin' in the clubs of Detroit as well as a debuted acting talent starring in her latest film, "One Last Flip" on Amazon Prime.

Big Fifty attributes her success to being a devout member of the Ifa faith and believes her ancestors guide her way through the future. She refuses to let the past dictate where she goes from here. Her latest project has proven that not even sky is the limit for her. She's at the top of her game!

Big Fifty now resides comfortably in the suburbs of Detroit, Michigan and enjoys spending time with her two grandsons, Kingston, 13 and Kamari, 11. She also enjoys her hobby of home decorating when she finds the time to do so.

AVAILABLE NOW

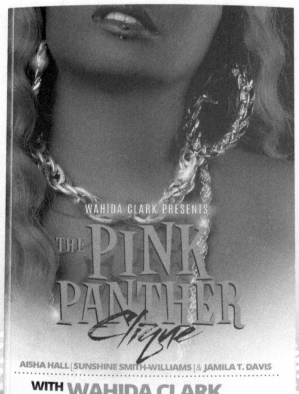

AVAILABLE NOW

FROM WAHIDA CLARK PRESENTS INNOVATIVE PUBLISHING

AVAILABLE NOW

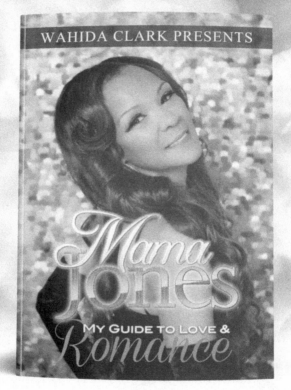

WAHIDA CLARK PRESENTS

Mama Jones

MY GUIDE TO LOVE & Romance

NEW RELEASE

WAHIDA CLARK PRESENTS

SECRET

DESIRES

OF THE ONE PERCENT:

A SHORT STORY COLLECTION FROM THE WORLD'S
MOST NOTORIOUS MADAM
...

ANNA GRISTINA

i WAHIDA CLARK
PRESENTS
INNOVATIVE PUBLISHING

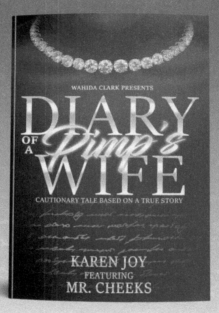

CPSIA information can be obtained
at www.ICGtesting.com
Printed in the USA
LVHW041755280722
724566LV00005B/82